TRIUMPH
B O O K S
542 South Dearborn Street, Suite 750
Chicago, Illinois 60605
www.triumphbooks.com

Pojo's 2006 Yu-Gi-Oh! Annual Table of Contents

Table of Contents - Credits

Credits

Editor in Chief ....Bill Gill, a.k.a. "Pojo"
Creative Director.............Jon Anderson, a.k.a. "JonnyO"
Project Manager ....Bob Baker, a.k.a. "BB Gun"
Contributors....................Jae Kim, Evan Vargas, Adam Povey, Michael Lucas, Jason Cohen, Mike Rosenberg, George Niederhofer, Wicked, Snapper, Coin Flip, Darrel Dorigatti, Ken Hartwick, Joseph Lee, Ricky Riles, Baz Griffiths, and Amy Gill.

pojo.com
When it's not just a game!

Holy Obelisk, the Tormentor! It's time for yet another Yu-Gi-Oh! Annual!

It's 2006, and Yu-Gi-Oh! is still chugging along. The original Yu-Gi-Oh! anime (cartoon), Duel Monsters, wraps up this year. We will be saying farewell to Yugi, Joey, Seto, Tristan & Tea in 2006. At least for the foreseeable future.

But the Yu-Gi-Oh! franchise isn't being forgotten. It's just steering in a new direction. A new Yu-Gi-Oh! anime started airing in the Fall of 2005: *Yu-Gi-Oh! GX.* GX takes place after the Duel Monsters storyline ends. Seto Kaiba has opened up a Duelist Academy, and students stay in dorms named after the Egyptian God Cards. (Sound Harry Potter-ish to anyone else out there?). I like the change in direction. Guys like Yugi & Goku can only save the world so many times before it becomes pretty lame.

The card game also continues to flourish. *Konami & Upper Deck* came out with a new Banned/Restricted list in the Fall of 2005 to keep the game from getting stagnant. Some powerful cards were placed on the Banned List allowing for Deck Builders to come up with a whole new breed of winning decks. The Advanced Format is looking awesome for 2006. Konami is also steering Yu-Gi-Oh! Trading Cards in a new direction. The anime characters like Yugi & Kaiba are being removed from card packaging, and being replaced with monsters. Konami knows that kids love monsters.

With all these changes happening, our Yu-Gi-Oh! Annual for 2006 is perfectly timed this year.

I've spoken to many folks on the *www.pojo.com* message boards, at tournaments, and via email. You always tell me what you want to see in books. Mostly I hear: *"More Killer Decks".* So this time, we have the largest Killer Decks section ever! The Killer Decks Section is over 40 pages long, and covers 20 different deck ideas from our Pros.

What else will you find inside?

- *Top 10 Lists*
- *Strategies for Deck Building*
- *Yu-Gi-Oh! GX Season 1 summary*
- *Puzzles, Video Game Reviews, and a whole lot more.*

3

The Advanced Format – The Limited List
Also known as the Banned/Restricted List

There are two basic formats you can play in constructed Yugioh Events: **Advanced and Traditional**.

In simple terms, there are **no forbidden cards** in the Traditional Format. You can play with all your favorite cards. Many people do not like playing in the Traditional Format. Why Not? Too many cards are *"Broken*"*.

The Advanced Format is the favorite amongst expert Duelists. Game Play is more challenging. Deck Building is also more challenging. There are a greater variety of decks being played in the Advanced Format due to the Banned & Restricted Cards.

Upper Deck uses the Advanced Format at Regional Events, National Events, and the World Championship. It is the format that **we recommend** you play as well.

The Pojo Dictionary:

* Broken = Cards that are simply too good and too powerful. Broken Cards are usually banned or restricted to make game play more enjoyable. Example: "Pot of Greed is Broken."

4

The Advanced Format – The Forbidden List
Effective October 1, 2005

I. Forbidden Cards
You cannot use these cards in your Deck, Fusion Deck or Side Deck.

- Black Luster Soldier - Envoy of the Beginning
- Butterfly Dagger - Elma
- Change of Heart
- Chaos Emperor Dragon - Envoy of the End
- Delinquent Duo
- Fiber Jar
- Graceful Charity
- Harpie's Feather Duster
- Imperial Order
- Magical Scientist
- Makyura the Destructor
- Mirage of Nightmare
- Mirror Force
- Monster Reborn
- Painful Choice
- Pot of Greed
- Raigeki
- Ring of Destruction
- Sinister Serpent
- The Forceful Sentry
- Tribe-Infecting Virus
- Witch of the Black Forest
- Yata-Garasu

II. Limited Cards
You can ONLY use one of the following cards in the Deck, Fusion Deck & Side Deck combined.

- Book of Moon
- Book of Taiyou
- Breaker the Magical Warrior
- Call of the Haunted
- Card Destruction
- Ceasefire
- Confiscation
- Cyber Jar
- D. D. Warrior Lady
- Dark Hole
- Dark Magician of Chaos
- Deck Devastation Virus
- Exchange of the Spirit (Available at Shonen Jump's Elemental Energy Sneak Preview!)
- Exiled Force
- Exodia the Forbidden One
- Heavy Storm
- Injection Fairy Lily
- Jinzo
- Left Arm of the Forbidden One
- Left Leg of the Forbidden One
- Lightning Vortex
- Limiter Removal
- Mage Power
- Magic Cylinder
- Magician of Faith
- Metamorphosis
- Morphing Jar
- Mystical Space Typhoon
- Night Assailant
- Nobleman of Crossout
- Premature Burial
- Protector of the Sanctuary
- Reckless Greed
- Reflect Bounder
- Right Arm of the Forbidden One
- Right Leg of the Forbidden One
- Sacred Phoenix of Nephthys
- Sangan
- Scapegoat
- Snatch Steal
- Swords of Revealing Light
- Thousand-Eyes Restrict
- Torrential Tribute
- Tsukuyomi
- Twin-Headed Behemoth
- United We Stand

III. Semi-Limited Cards
You can ONLY use two of the following cards in the Deck, Fusion Deck & Side Deck combined.

- Abyss Soldier
- Creature Swap
- Emergency Provisions
- Good Goblin Housekeeping
- Gravity Bind
- Last Turn
- Level Limit - Area B
- Manticore of Darkness
- Reinforce- ment of the Army
- Upstart Goblin

The Traditional Format – The Limited List

In simple terms, there are **no forbidden cards** in the Traditional Format. You can play with all your favorite cards. While the Advanced Format is the most popular tournament format for playing the Yu-Gi-Oh! Trading Cards Game, the Traditional Format still sees some casual play.

The Traditional Format allows you to play with **fun cards** you may not have used in a while, like: *Pot of Greed, Black Luster Soldier, Yata-Garasu, Monster Reborn*, etc. **Konami** has created this Limited List to make the Traditional Format Playing Environment as fair as possible.

While our book focuses more on the Advanced Format, we have a couple of **Killer Decks** inside based on the Traditional Format. Additionally, Ken Hartwick has strategy article regarding the Traditional Format as well.

The Traditional Format – The Limited List
Effective October 1, 2005

I. Forbidden Cards
There are no Forbidden Cards in this format.

II. Limited Cards
You can ONLY use one of the following cards in the Deck, Fusion Deck or Side Deck combined:

- Black Luster Soldier - Envoy of the Beginning
- Book of Moon
- Book of Taiyou
- Breaker the Magical Warrior
- Butterfly Dagger - Elma
- Call of the Haunted
- Card Destruction
- Ceasefire
- Change of Heart
- Chaos Emperor Dragon - Envoy of the End
- Confiscation
- Cyber Jar
- D. D. Warrior Lady
- Dark Hole
- Dark Magician of Chaos
- Deck Devastation Virus
- Delinquent Duo
- Exchange of the Spirit (Available at Shonen Jump's Elemental Energy Sneak Preview!)
- Exiled Force
- Exodia the Forbidden One
- Fiber Jar
- Graceful Charity
- Harpie's Feather Duster

- Heavy Storm
- Imperial Order
- Injection Fairy Lily
- Jinzo
- Left Arm of the Forbidden One
- Left Leg of the Forbidden One
- Lightning Vortex
- Limiter Removal
- Mage Power
- Magic Cylinder
- Magical Scientist
- Makyura the Destructor
- Metamorphosis
- Mirage of Nightmare
- Mirror Force
- Monster Reborn
- Morphing Jar
- Mystical Space Typhoon
- Night Assailant
- Painful Choice
- Pot of Greed
- Premature Burial
- Protector of the Sanctuary
- Raigeki
- Reckless Greed
- Reflect Bounder
- Right Arm of the Forbidden One
- Right Leg of the Forbidden One
- Ring of Destruction
- Sacred Phoenix of Nephthys
- Sangan

- Scapegoat
- Sinister Serpent
- Snatch Steal
- Swords of Revealing Light
- The Forceful Sentry
- Thousand-Eyes Restrict
- Torrential Tribute
- Tribe-Infecting Virus
- Tsukuyomi
- Twin-Headed Behemoth
- United We Stand
- Witch of the Black Forest
- Yata-Garasu

III. Semi-Limited Cards
You can ONLY use two of the following cards in the Deck, Fusion Deck or Side Deck combined:

- Abyss Soldier
- Creature Swap
- Emergency Provisions
- Good Goblin Housekeeping
- Gravity Bind
- Last Turn
- Level Limit - Area B
- Manticore of Darkness
- Nobleman of Crossout
- Reinforcement of the Army
- Upstart Goblin

2006 Pojo's Yu-Gi-Oh! ANNUAL

KILLER DECKS
from the crew of
Pojo.com

Spellcaster Traditional Killer Deck
Traditional Format

By: Evan Vargas a.k.a "SandTrap"

Want the perfect deck to take out all the other Chaos decks in the format? Put your faith into the power of *Spellcasters* to lead you to victory! But this is no normal Spellcaster deck – it's got a trick up its sleeve.

The trump card is the trap known as *Magician's Circle*. Whenever a Spellcaster-type monster attacks, Magician's Circle can be activated to special summon a Spellcaster with 2000 ATK or less from each player's deck to the field.

With Magician's Circle, you can force your opponent to waste valuable monsters while tearing apart their hand, thanks to the support of White Magical Hat! Magician's Circle forces both monsters summoned to go into face-up ATK position, and most players stick with Magical Scientist and Magician of Faith for their Spellcasters. Here's where you'll have the advantage; by special summoning White Magical Hat, you'll be able to attack that Scientist or Magician of Faith without their effects activated, all the while nailing a card from your opponent's hand, and thus limiting his or her options. Once you press your advantage with White Magical Hat a couple times, you should have little trouble to deal with as your coast your way to a win!

Monsters -17-

[3] Kycoo the Ghost Destroyer
[2] Skilled Dark Magician
[2] White Magical Hat
[2] Magician of Faith
[1] Magical Scientist
[1] D.D. Warrior Lady
[1] Chaos Emperor Dragon – Envoy of the End
[1] Witch of the Black Forest
[1] Sangan
[1] Sinister Serpent
[1] Yata-Garasu
[1] Fiber Jar

Spells -16-

[1] Pot of Greed
[1] Graceful Charity
[1] Painful Choice
[1] Delinquent Duo
[1] The Forceful Sentry
[1] Harpie's Feather Duster
[1] Heavy Storm
[1] Mystical Space Typhoon
[1] Raigeki
[1] Dark Hole
[1] Change of Heart
[1] Monster Reborn
[1] Premature Burial
[1] Snatch Steal
[2] Nobleman of Crossout

Traps -7-

[1] Imperial Order
[1] Ring of Destruction
[1] Mirror Force
[1] Call of the Haunted
[1] Torrential Tribute
[2] Magician's Circle

Destructive Exchange
Traditional Format

By: Mike "Dawn Yoshi" Rosenberg

Makyura the Destructor makes "Destructive Exchange" a possible first-turn kill deck

There's nothing more ***ridiculous*** than a first-turn-kill deck. Every duelist will tell you that. Even the duelists who pilot first-turn-kill decks will tell you that! The ability to defeat your opponent before they can even draw their first card is something the advanced format tries to avoid. It's not always possible, as creative and diabolical duelists will always try to find the next big combo deck, but the updates to the advanced format's forbidden list attempts to do away with the silliness of basically playing solitaire with your opponent.

However, the traditional format is plentiful in very silly cards. Any format in which you can play ***Raige-ki*** should allow some of the most insane decks to roam free. Thanks to the Elemental Energy sneak preview events, Exchange of the Spirit has been introduced into the traditional environment. Exchange of the Spirit allows you to switch both

Monsters: 9

Thunder Dragon x3
Cyber Jar
Morphing Jar
Makyura the Destructor
Magician of Faith x3

Spells: 20

Pot of Greed
Graceful Charity
Painful Choice
Book of Taiyou
Book of Moon
Upstart Goblin x2
Reasoning x3
Card Destruction
Serial Spell x2
Toon Table of Contents x3
Soul Release x2
A Feather of the Phoenix x3

Traps: 10

Exchange of the Spirit
Jar of Greed x3
Good Goblin Housekeeping x2
Desert Sunlight x2
Reckless Greed

players' decks with their respective graveyards, as long as you meet the activation condition of having **15 or more cards** in your graveyard. So, what exactly happens if your opponent has no cards in their graveyard when you activate this? To summarize what happens, **when you activate Exchange of the Spirit, your opponent basically loses the duel,** as they will have no cards to draw during their next draw phase. That is the true power of *"Destructive Exchange".*

Your Goal

Makyura the Destructor makes "Destructive Exchange" a possible first-turn-kill deck, as its ability allows you to activate Exchange of the Spirit during your turn. However, it also allows you to cycle through your deck with a variety of card-drawing trap cards, such as *Jar of Greed* and *Good Goblin Housekeeping*. **Your most important goal** is to send Makyura the Destructor to the graveyard as soon as possible,

as it's the easiest method for you to win the duel with this deck. ***The best methods of thinning your deck are with*** *Cyber Jar, Reasoning,* **and** *Painful Choice,* which fill up your graveyard at an incredibly fast pace. These cards also add to your combo's consistency, and will allow you to dig through your deck with even more options. Reasoning, however, can send that one copy of Exchange of the Spirit to the graveyard. This is why A Feather of the Phoenix is **crucial,** as it allows you to return your win condition to your hand with the help of some card drawing.

The Follow Through

The rest of this deck consists of any method that can thin your deck or fill up your graveyard, as these cards help you achieve that 15 card requirement to activating Exchange of the Spirit even **faster.** Soul Release, as the last back-up option, allows you to remove any

cards that may have ended up in your opponent's graveyard through effects such as Card Destruction or Morphing Jar.

In an environment of silly combos and powerful effects, decks based on Exchange of the Spirit have earned their place at the top of the traditional format. After all, who needs Yata-Garasu when you can make your opponent deck-out in one turn?

11

Soul Control
Advanced Format

By: Evan Vargas a.k.a "SandTrap"

T ired of running the same old cookie cutter? Perhaps it's time to try out a deck that I pioneered at the **Pomona Shonen Jump Championship** – Soul Control. First, we'll take a look at the new, updated deck list for the current Advanced Format, and then discuss the strategy and how to play Soul Control. With some practice, you'll be winning your next tournament in no time at all!

Gravekeeper's Spy will help maintain field presence and give extra tribute fodder for the powerful Monarchs

The main strategy behind Soul Control (as well as the reason behind the name of the deck) involves using a special combo to gain card advantage over your opponent. When you have card advantage, you'll have a higher chance of winning the duel.

Soul Exchange is the main card of the combo. Coming out of the first Yugi Starter Deck, it's an old card that's found new use lately.

Get Control

Activate Soul Exchange on one of your opponent's monster, and tribute it for your own monster – mainly Thestalos the Firestorm Monarch, or Mobius the Frost Monarch. Soul Exchange effectively destroyed your opponent's monster, so that's a one-for-one trade. Thestalos is summoned to the field at no cost, but then activates its special effect, taking a card away from the opponent's hand, thus a **1-for-0 trade.** So after Thestalos is summoned, you've got yourself a two-for-one combo that puts you ahead of your opponent!

The same results can happen when using Mobius instead of Thestalos. After playing Soul Exchange, tribute for Mobius the Frost Monarch and nail up to two Spell or Trap cards for a possible three-for-one combo! Brain Control **can't** target face-down

Monsters: 18

[3] Thestalos the Firestorm Monarch
[2] Mobius the Frost Monarch
[2] Apprentice Magician
[2] Old Vindictive Magician
[1] Magician of Faith
[2] Gravekeeper's Spy
[3] D.D. Assailant
[1] D.D. Warrior Lady
[1] Breaker the Magical Warrior
[1] Sangan

Spells: 14

[1] Confiscation
[1] Dark Hole
[1] Heavy Storm
[1] Mystical Space Typhoon
[1] Snatch Steal
[1] Premature Burial
[1] Book of Moon
[1] Nobleman of Crossout
[2] Smashing Ground
[2] Brain Control
[2] Soul Exchange

Traps: 8

[1] Torrential Tribute
[1] Call of the Haunted
[2] Dust Tornado
[2] Sakuretsu Armor
[2] Bottomless Trap Hole

monsters, but it can still take face-up ones. With Brain Control, you could take an opponent's monster, tribute for Mobius, destroy two Spell or Trap cards, and then attack another of your opponent's monsters for a tremendous four-for-one combo! Incredible!

Watch Out

You may not draw into a Soul Exchange or Brain Control when you need it. When that happens, don't worry; the monster and trap line-up helps to support the Monarchs and makes it easy to tribute for your big hitters without the help of Spell cards.

For example, take a look at *Apprentice Magician*. Your opponent's D.D. Assailant just crashed into your Magician, so via the monster's effect, Special Summon Old Vindictive Magician to the field. Next turn, Flip Summon your new magician to destroy D.D. Assailant, and then tribute the *now-useless monster* for Thestalos or Mobius for more card advantage!

Gravekeeper's Spy will help maintain field presence and give extra tribute fodder for the powerful Monarchs, while Spirit Reaper will stay on the field for an extended amount of time, thanks to its effect. Don't forget the Trap cards that can help destroy the

opponent's monsters and help keep your monsters alive so they may be sacrificed next turn for whichever Monarch would hurt the opponent the most at that time. With a plethora of **card advantage** opportunities and plenty of support cards to make sure they work, Soul Control may just be the deck you've been waiting for.

13

Zombie Decks in the New Format
Advanced Format

By: Jae Love

For those who want to add some *Zombie Madness* to the new format, here it is!

Monsters

The monster lineup focuses on the tremendous power of Ryu Kokki, which is now unquestionably the best tribute monster among Zombies. It can ram into a Mirror Walled D.D Assailant and take it down! It also trades with Injection Fairy Lily and laughs at Cyber Dragon's puny 2100 attack score.

Goblin Elite Attack Force is **great** against your opponent's strategy as well, and will be helped by the inclusion of a Gigantes be-cause of the numerous Earth monsters in the deck. All of the Earth monsters, almost, can be searched by Giant Rat as well, creating great synergy among the parts.

Rat can go into either heavy field presence with Lily, monster removal with Exiled Force, or *any zombie with Pyramid Turtle.* Use it to your advantage with a spell lineup that exploits the Rat's power!

Spells

All of the staples are accounted for. To add spice to the proceedings, two copies of Creature Swap will help cycle

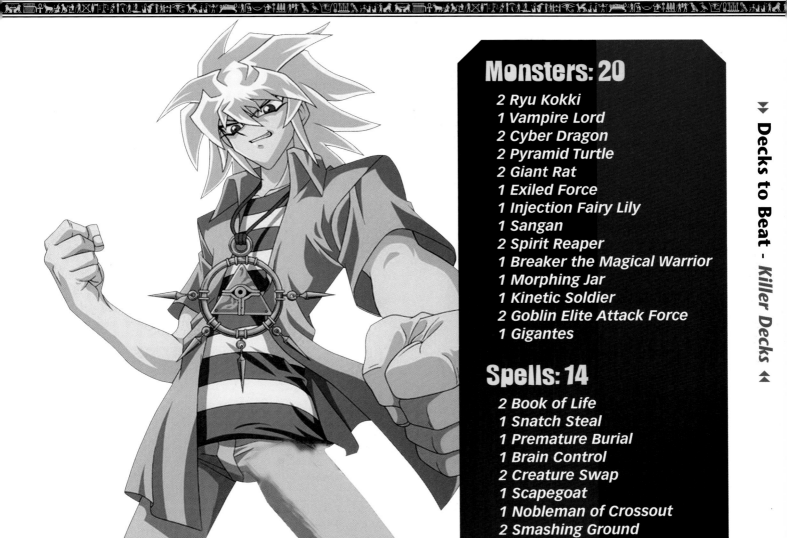

Monsters: 20

2 Ryu Kokki
1 Vampire Lord
2 Cyber Dragon
2 Pyramid Turtle
2 Giant Rat
1 Exiled Force
1 Injection Fairy Lily
1 Sangan
2 Spirit Reaper
1 Breaker the Magical Warrior
1 Morphing Jar
1 Kinetic Soldier
2 Goblin Elite Attack Force
1 Gigantes

Spells: 14

2 Book of Life
1 Snatch Steal
1 Premature Burial
1 Brain Control
2 Creature Swap
1 Scapegoat
1 Nobleman of Crossout
2 Smashing Ground
1 Heavy Storm
1 Dark Hole
1 Mystical Space Typhoon

Traps: 8

3 Dust Tornado
1 Torrential Tribute
1 Call of the Haunted
1 Robbin Goblin
2 Sakuretsu Armor

out those Giant Rats and Pyramid Turtles for optimal effects. You can immediately junction from a Pyramid Turtle into a Spirit Reaper, then use Smashing Ground or Brain Control to try to discard a card from your opponent's hand. There are a lot of possibilities with this killer zombie deck.

Traps

This trap lineup evokes memories of my Charlotte ***Shonen Jump Championship*** deck. This deck will use three copies of Dust Tornado to ensure the heavy Zombie hitters will arrive onto the field.

Robbin Goblin and Call of the Haunted have great synergy with the card, and ***two copies of** Sakuretsu Armor* will provide all of the defense we'll likely need. Have fun playing with this Zombie deck and good luck unleashing the power of this build!

The Aggro Warrior Toolbox
A Reinforced Army Beats Down Opponents!
Advanced Format

By: Michael Lucas

Warriors have almost always been a driving force in Yu-Gi-Oh. From Marauding Captain in Legacy of Darkness, to Don Zaloog and his discards in PGD, and who can forget the ever-present *Black Luster Soldier – Envoy of the Beginning* we've dealt with up through the end of September of 2005? Even without the Soldier, the changes to the new Forbidden and Restricted lists give the Warrior deck a big boost. Here's an example of a deck that focuses on **using the search-ability and raw power** of several Warrior monsters to take down opponents in short order, with a couple extra tricks up its sleeve:

Monsters:

The deck contains a fairly solid build of warriors. The 3 DD Assailants and lone DD Warrior Lady offer some consistency in the ability to remove opposing monsters from the game. The **Command**

Knights are a great opening set with their 1900 defense, and help to power up your other warriors when going on the offensive. *Blade Knight* is not only a solid attacker, but he will get his attack boost quite often, as cards in hand tend to run out quickly in the new format. *Don Zaloogs* provide a healthy dose of hand discard, *Goblin Attack Force* takes out an opposing Cyber Dragon or Vampire Lord, and Exiled Force gets rid of a scary face-down that could wreck your game if it was flipped. The deck is packing the standard Breaker, Magician and Sangan, but two things that might be a surprise are the 3 Cyber Dragons and the Drillroid. Even though the deck is based on Warriors, the Cyber Dragons add speed to the deck, hence why it's an Aggro/Warrior deck. The Drillroid dispatches enemy Spirit Reapers and other face-downs (but sadly, he can't stop flips.)

Spells:

Most of these spells are standard to all decks now; you'll most likely find Heavy Storm, Mystical Space Typhoon, Dark Hole, a couple of Smashing Grounds, Nobleman of Crossout, Scapegoat, Book of Moon, Premature Burial, and Snatch Steal in 90% of decks; with almost any deck, the spell/trap destruction, monster destruction, defense, and revival these cards provide **will be vital**. However, this deck has a few cards that can't be thrown into anything. *2 Reinforcements of the Army gives the deck its versatility,* pulling the right warrior for the right situation. Have an open field to hit? Grab Don Zaloog for a hand

Monsters: 18

3x D. D. Assailant
3x Cyber Dragon
2x Command Knight
2x Don Zaloog
1x Goblin Attack Force
1x Blade Knight
1x D. D. Warrior Lady
1x Exiled Force
1x Breaker the Magical Warrior
1x Drillroid
1x Sangan
1x Magician of Faith

Spells: 15

2x Reinforcement of the Army
1x Heavy Storm
1x Mystical Space Typhoon
1x Dark Hole
2x Smashing Ground
1x Nobleman of Crossout
1x Scapegoat
1x Book of Moon
1x Premature Burial
1x Snatch Steal
1x Swords of Revealing Light
1x Confiscation
1x Wave Motion Cannon

Traps: 8

3x Sakuretsu Armor
1x Bottomless Trap Hole
2x Dust Tornado
1x Call of the Haunted
1x Torrential Tribute

Sidedeck:

2x Mataza the Zapper
1x Mobius the Frost Monarch
1x Morphing Jar
1x Mystic Swordsman Lv. 2
1x Giant Trunade
1x United We Stand
1x Wave Motion Cannon
1x Ceasefire
1x Dust Tornado
2x Solemn Judgment
3x Waboku

discard. Your opponent have a really strong monster out? Grab DD Assailant and ram it into them. Your opponent has a face-down that might be a Cyber or Morphing Jar? Exiled Force will put a quick stop to that. The other big stand-out is **Wave-Motion Cannon.** This card can punish your opponent for playing their Spell/Trap removal too early or win a game where you only need a little more damage.

Traps:

There's not much to say as there aren't many Traps. The Sakuretsus get rid of powerful opposing monsters, as does a Bot-tomless Trap Hole played at the right time. *Call of the Haunted and Torrential Tribute are automatic inclusions* in almost every deck, and the Dust Tornadoes clear out potential threats to your monsters.

Overall, the deck does very well. A very similar version of this deck took *1st place* at the recent *Regional tournament in Butler, PA* (won by Ben Coburn). The quick field swarm from Cyber Dragons and the consistency that Reinforcements of the Army provides will give any opponent trouble, and completely obliterate those unprepared for it. Why not give a Warrior deck a try and see how well it does for you?

17

Constructing the Dark Paladin Spellcaster Deck

Advanced Format

By: **Dark Paladin aka Alex Searcy**

First, let's talk a little about the focal monster of the deck: *Dark Paladin*.

Dark Paladin
Level 8
2900-2400
Dark/Spellcaster

This card can **only be Special Summoned by** *Fusion Summon*. As long as this card remains face up on the field, you can negate the activation of one Spell card and destroy it by discarding one card from your hand.

The attack of this card increases by 500 points for every **Dragon** on the field and in either player's Graveyard.

What You'll Need

Now, let's look at the monster necessary for this deck, starting with tribute monsters.

Dark Magician of Chaos is an excellent asset to the deck. 2800 attack is very solid and he has a couple of bonuses. First, when Normal summoned, you can retrieve a Spell from your Graveyard. He also removes from play all the monsters he destroys. *Jinzo* is included obviously to help nutrilize trap threats while Dark Magician is required to summon Dark Paladin.

NOTE: *You can use Dark Magician OR Buster Blader (I prefer to use Dark Magician, at least here, as this is a Spellcaster deck.)*

Ban list compliant as

of October 1st for the

Advanced Format.

Fusion Monsters x2

Dark Paladin x2
Tribute Monsters x4
Dark Magician of Chaos
Dark Magician x2
Jinzo
Non-Tribute Monsters x12
King of the Swamp x3
Breaker the Magical Warrior
Skilled Dark Magician x3
Sangan
Magician of Faith
DD Warrior Lady
Cyber Jar
Morphing Jar

Spell Cards x17

Swords of Revealing Light
Polymerization x2
Different Dimension Capsule
Mystic Plasma Zone
Big Bang Shot
Scapegoat
Premature Burial
Mystical Space Typhoon
Dark Hole
Confiscation
Heavy Storm
Card Destruction
Cost Down
Enemy Controller
Mage Power
Lightning Vortex

Traps x7

Dust Tornado
Magic Cylinder
Ceasefire
Torrential Tribute
Call of the Haunted
Divine Wrath
Waboku

King of the Swamp is our Fusion Substitute used in place of Buster Blader. He can also be used to retrieve Polymerization from the deck.

Breaker **and** ***Skilled Dark Magician*** **are staples in this deck.** Magician of Faith is for the Spell re-use and the two Jars are for hand and field replenishment. DD Warrior Lady adds some removal and Sangan can bring out most of these monsters.

What to Add

Of course, your Spell staples (MST, Dark Hole, Confiscation, and Heavy Storm) are here. The rest of these Spells are either to power up your monsters or add a little destruction to your opponent (such as Lightning Vortex). ***Different Dimension Capsule*** is there for a little extra draw power with Graceful banned and Scapegoat adds a little protection.

In our traps, we have protection with Waboku and revival with Call of the Haunted. Some burn with Cylinder and Ceasefire and field destruction with Torrential Tribute, Dust Tornado, and Divine Wrath.

New Age Chaos!
Advanced Format

By: Ricky "RJ" Riles

I picked out New Age Chaos as my *"Killer Deck"* for this book, I felt that it would be cool to write about the deck that never wants to go away, Chaos. Chaos has been around since it was released in *"Invasion of Chaos,"* obviously, and it has lived on through each and every banned list. Much to the dismay of Yu-Gi-Oh! Players everywhere.

The Chaos Monsters were so popular because not only were they ***incredibly easy to summon,*** with just a Light and Dark monster in your graveyard, but because their effects were so powerful. Often referred to as the best cards in the entire game!

Get Some Chaos

Now, the only thing we have that is Chaos is *Chaos Sorcerer*. The worst Chaos monster, but it's VERY good, so that says A LOT about chaos, even the worst of them are playable! In this particular deck, I utilize Chaos Sorcerer with the absolutely broken, *Cyber Dragon*. With Cyber Dragon being not only a Light type monster, but having amazing Stats and Effect, any deck

17 Monsters

1 Chaos Sorcerer
2 Cyber Dragon
1 Ninja Grandmaster Sasuke
1 D.D. Warrior Lady
1 Magician of Faith
1 Breaker the Magical Warrior
1 Don Zaloog
1 Sangan
2 Spirit Reaper
3 D.D. Assailant
1 Mobius the Frost Monarch
1 Exiled Force
1 Injection Fairy Lily

16 Spells

1 Dark Hole
1 Confiscation
1 Heavy Storm
1 Mystical Space Typhoon
1 Snatch Steal
1 Premature Burial
2 Smashing Ground
2 Enemy Controller
1 Scapegoat
1 Book of Moon
1 Metamorphosis
1 Reinforcement of the Army
1 Nobleman of Crossout
1 Swords of Revealing Light

7 Traps

3 Sakuretsu Armor
2 Widespread Ruin
1 Torrential Tribute
1 Call of The Haunted

Total: 40 Cards

that has Chaos Sorcerer, in my opinion, should pack some Cyber Dragons to go along with it.

Add Some Lights

We still need about three more lights, so I go with **D.D. Warrior Lady, Ninja Grandmaster Sasuke, and Magician of Faith.** All have nice effects, although Magician of Faith is kind of "so-so," I like it somewhat in this deck. Ninja works with the 2 Enemy Controllers, as well as having a nice 1800 Attack. Our Dark monsters consist of **2 Spirit Reapers, Breaker, Don Zaloog, and Sangan.** We have the almost staple (For CC) 3 D.D. Assailants, and our one tribute monster is **Mobius the Frost Monarch.** Rounded out with **Exiled Force, and Injection Fairy Lily.**

The monsters are...basically all the normal ones. Dark Hole, Confiscation, Heavy, MST, Premature, and Snatch Steal. They are, to me, semi staples. We have even more removal in 2 Smashing Ground. Enemy Controller is "Decree Ready Defense," and the other ef-

fect can be a game winner, sometimes.

My traps are chocked full of removal! I love a lot of removal, and this trap line-up is full of it. Every card removes something from the field, with the exception of Call of The Haunted, but that can bring back Chaos Sorcerer, and Exiled Force etc.

Now Some Removal

This all leads to, you guessed it, **More Removal!**

This deck isn't something I would bring to a **Shonen Jump Tournament,** but it IS a great thing to work off of if you are building your own deck, possibly your first deck, if you are a newbie. In this state, it is quite solid, with a bit of skill, and practice, you should be able to do VERY well in a local tournament, unless you go to some insane tournament like **Comic Odyssey,** but that's not very likely :).

By the way, you WILL need a side deck and a Fusion deck.

I included **Metamorphosis** in the deck. Its only one Morph though, but with Magician of Faith, you should probably have two of everything, if allowed.

21

Freed and Co.
Advanced Format

By: Ryoga (Adam Povey)

Warriors are the best *"type"* in Yu-Gi-Oh. They have the strongest *"tutor"* (card for searching your deck for a card), creating a toolbox of monsters for any situation. This deck deals with the more obscure *"Light Warriors"*. They were mostly used to summon Chaos monsters, but prove their worth here.

Freed the Brave Wanderer is one of the more useful cards in the deck. All you need is two Light monsters in your Graveyard and **any large monster can be gone!** 1700 ATK takes down everything else. Where will these Light monsters come from? **Thunder Dragon, Card Destruction, and Morphing Jar!** Thunder Dragon thins your deck, making it more likely to draw a powerful card and the others reset your hand. **Magical Merchant and Magician of Faith** provide defence and replenish your hand.

> Freed the Brave Wanderer is one of the more useful cards in the deck.

Cyber Dragon is the most powerful card in the new format. It *"swarms"* (bring out many mon-sters in one turn) effectively and, being Light, provides fodder for Freed. **You should never Tribute Summon it.** Save him until you can use that effect! Also, go second whenever possible, so he can bait out your opponent's defences, allowing you to win faster.

The remaining monsters build the *'Warrior Toolbox'* held together by Reinforcement of the Army. In the early game, **Blade Knight** eliminates pesky Flip Effect monsters and works later as a *"beatstick"* (big monster). **Exiled Force and D. D. Warrior Lady** are monster destroyers to order and **Don Zaloog** adds a pinch of control to clinch victory. Good side decks are D. D. Assailant for extra monster removal, Zombyra the Dark, another Blade Knight, and even Thunder Nyan Nyan could be added for extra aggression, and Mystic Swordsman LV2 destroys annoying Mystic Tomatoes, Stealth Birds, and Pyramid Turtles.

I admit the traps are stereotyped, but they work. I use Sakuretsu Armor over Bottomless Trap Hole for **two reasons:**

1. It is a better "topdeck" (card you draw when you have no other cards).

2. It can stop Kinetic Soldier, scourge of existence (from a Warrior Point of View anyway).

Dust Tornado could be added to deal with burn and Sakuretsu Armors and for another way to win, you could throw in Return from the *Different Dimension.* The Spells are the remaining staples, with My Body as a Shield to counter inconveniently timed Dark Holes. Luminous Spark is a personal touch. It adds that little ATK needed to finish the game. However, it is liable to destruction, so use it carefully.

This deck should be played aggressively. The exces-sive monster destruction is designed to make sure your opponent never gains field advantage (having more cards on the field then you). Don Zaloog and Magical Merchant were added for consistency, but can be taken out for more aggressive monsters. This deck has done well in play testing, but still has a long way to go. Pick it up, try it out, and be creative! You never know what you might find.

Monsters 19:

Freed the Brave Wanderer X3
Thunder Dragon X3
Cyber Dragon X3
Breaker the Magical Warrior X1
Sangan X1
Morphing Jar X1
D. D. Warrior Lady X1
Exiled Force X1
Magician of Faith X1
Blade Knight X2
Don Zaloog X1
Magical Merchant X1

Spells 17:

Dark Hole X1
Snatch Steal X1
Premature Burial X1
Mystical Space Typhoon X1
Confiscation X1
Reinforcement of the Army X2
Heavy Storm X1
Scapegoat X1
Card Destruction X1
Nobleman of Crossout X1
Swords of Revealing Light X1
Book of Moon X1
Smashing Ground X2
My Body as a Shield X1
Luminous Spark X1

Traps 4:

Call of the Haunted X1
Torrential Tribute X1
Sakuretsu Armor X2

23

Decks to Beat - *Killer Decks*

Building a Successful Fiend Deck
Advanced Format

By: George Niederhofer a.k.a. YamiBakuraFan

Since the early days of the Yu-Gi-Oh! Trading card game there has always been a sinister and powerful deck type that has stood out among the rest to me. This would be the *fiend deck*. I have been playing in tournaments with many versions of fiend decks since it became a viable deck type at the release of the *Labyrinth of Nightmare* booster set.

A certain card was released among that set that would single-handedly create the fiend deck. This card was *Dark Necrofear; a monster like no other. Wow!* A non tribute 2200 *"Beat-stick"* that can transform into a human Snatch Steal? I couldn't say no to it. Even today, some eleven booster sets later, Dark Necrofear remains a potent card in the play environment and still merits a deck built around it. Today I will construct such a deck.

Another card commonly played in most Fiend decks would be *Dark Ruler Ha Des*. If Necrofear pioneered the fiend deck, Ha Des furthered the concept. With his negation ability and high attack he makes a great counterpart to Necrofear. ***Every fiend deck should have one to two Ha Des and Necrofear.*** These cards are basically what the fiend deck is about.

24

The Fiend Control Deck

2 **Dark Necrofear**
1 **Dark Ruler Ha Des**
3 **Slate Warrior**
2 **Mystic Tomato**
3 **Giant Germ**
2 **Dark Jeroid**
2 **Newdoria**
1 **Morphing Jar**
1 **Sangan**
1 **Night Assailant**
1 **Card Destruction**
1 **Dark Hole**
1 **Heavy Storm**
1 **Mystical Space Typhoon**
1 **Confiscation**
2 **Creature Swap**
1 **Snatch Steal**
1 **Premature Burial**
1 **Book of Moon**
1 **Scapegoat**
1 **Enemy Controller**
1 **Metamorphisis**
1 **Swords of Revealing Light**
1 **Nobleman of Crossout**
2 **Sakuretsu Armor**
1 **Torrential Tribute**
1 **Call of the Haunted**
2 **Dust Tornado**
1 **Mirror Wall**

There are tons of huge fiend beat sticks to choose from. We have *Giant Orcs, Slate Warriors, Archfiend Soldiers,* **and** *Goblin Elite Forces* for the offensive power. This is actually a greater amount of power hitters than any other type of monster currently released. But is a fiend beat down ideal? It really depends on your personal play style. I personally, prefer the control variant that involves Mystic Tomato as a centerpiece.

With *Scapegoat* down to one per deck, *Creature Swap* is now an easily abused card throughout the game environment. Next, we have *Mystic Tomato*. While its not a fiend itself, it has the nifty ability to summon almost any kind of fiend you want to the field. This works as a deck thinner and maintains field presence for you, not to mention it can grab the right card for the right situation; and with a deck full of 1500 attack or lower DARK fiends, you'll have a bevy of choices at hand.

Newdoria, Dark Jeroid, even extra *"swarmage"* with *Giant Germs* can be useful in some situations. My fiend deck build is highly Tomato based and doesn't use any of the power attackers aside from Slate Warrior, who has a control element of its own. The following deck list is very similar to my ideal fiend deck under the new restrictions. This may not be the way you want to play the deck, but that's what makes this game so wonderful. You can play a deck type however you like with whatever cards you want.

25

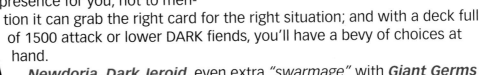

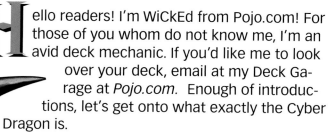

Cyber Dragons Attack!
Advanced Format

By: WiCkEd

Hello readers! I'm WiCkEd from Pojo.com! For those of you whom do not know me, I'm an avid deck mechanic. If you'd like me to look over your deck, email at my Deck Garage at *Pojo.com.* Enough of introductions, let's get onto what exactly the Cyber Dragon is.

Cyber Dragon, as you all may know, is one of the **most aggressive monsters played competitively today.** Its found its way into Aggro and Beatdown decks alike, more so, it can be thrown into almost any deck type and be successful. However, this is more about the dedicated Cyber Dragon deck. Of course it's going to include many things; Machines, Fusion, and a hint of cyber-ness that can only be found here in this very book.

Looking at Cyber Dragon he's a five-star 2100 attacker who is also Light. This is lovely in various ways, specifically the fact that his attack is very much so generous considering Cyber Dragon's effect. Alas, the Light Attribute is hand in hand with the Field Magic Luminous Spark, which adds 500 ATK points and detracts 400 DEF points. That's not important though, the REALLY good thing about Cyber Dragon is he's a Machine. This means Limiter Removal to double his attack then either end the game in a blow, or strike down something massive. Also for those of you who are unaware of this Dragon's effect, I'll explain it to you.

26

Cyber Dragon, as you all may know, is one of the most aggressive monsters played competitively today.

If your opponent happens to have one or more monsters on the field and you have none, **you can Special Summon it from your hand without having to tribute/sacrifice for it**. Very convenient. Also, to our added advantage, this brings the idea of Morph (using *Metamorphosis*) right after he is Special Summoned to change him into *Dark Balter the Terrible*. Or you could just attack with it and destroy whatever you wish on your opponents' field monster-wise. Entirely up to you, but with me, I enjoy the morph into Dark Balter.

So, thinking upon this Cyber Dragon is obviously a good card. That's nothing compared to *Cyber Twin Dragon* and *Cyber End Dragon,* the two fusions who follow the strain of Cyber Dragon. Cyber Twin Dragon itself is a level 8 Fusion Monster, his attack is 2800, and it can attack twice, which again, is quite the killer effect. Cyber End Dragon, the Level 12 Fusion monster with 4000 attack and *Trample is summonable via morph or the Fusion of 3, yes 3 Cyber Dragons.* Trample by the way, is slang for the *Fairy Meteor Crush effect* (when this card attacks a monster in defense position damage calculation applies normally).There is a possible simpler way to get out Cyber End Dragon, like Morph Koitsu into Cyber End. Koitsu though, is also Level 12. How does one get him out? Simple. Reasoning or Monster Gate. But, that's a WHOLE new deck archetype, so for those of you curious on the build of this deck, here is the list!

Monsters: 17

- 3 x Cyber Dragon
- 1 x Jinzo
- 1 x Breaker The Magical Warrior
- 1 x D.D. Warrior Lady
- 1 x Morphing Jar
- 1 x Sangan
- 1 x Magician of Faith
- 1 x Reflect Bounder
- 1 x Drilloid
- 1 x Cyber Stein
- 1 x Mystic Tomato
- 2 x X-Head Cannon
- 2 x Dekoichi the Battlechanted Locomotive

Magic/Spell: 17

- 1 x Dark Hole
- 1 x Heavy Storm
- 1 x Nobleman of Crossout
- 2 x Giant Trunade
- 1 x Power Bond
- 1 x Mystical Space Typhoon
- 1 x My Body As A Shield
- 1 x Snatch Steal
- 1 x Scapegoats
- 1 x Swords of Revealing Light
- 2 x Enemy Controller
- 1 x Book of Moon
- 1 x Limiter Removal
- 1 x Confiscation
- 1 x Wave-Motion Cannon

Traps: 6

- 2 x Dust Tornado
- 2 x Sakuretsu Armour
- 1 x Call of the Haunted
- 1 x Bottomless Trap Hole

27

Rentsy Deck
Advanced Format

By: Jason Cohen (a.k.a. Lord Tranorix)

Hello there, loyal readers, and welcome to my killer deck, which for lack of a better title, I shall call the *Rentsy Deck!*

It's a bit difficult to classify, but this is a deck that tries its best to maintain field control – although hand control certainly isn't ignored. There are elements of both *Burn* and *Beatdown* here, but I wouldn't consider the Rentsy Deck either one of them entirely.

> Giant Rat is a very versatile monster here.

Rentsy Stuff

Guardian Sphinx is the only tribute monster. With a powerful 2400 DEF, it has the ability to keep your opponent's field clean. Thanks to *Nobleman of Crossout's* being restricted to one in this format, Sphinx is better than he used to be.

Giant Rat is a very versatile monster here. He can search out Des Lacooda for one of the best combos in this deck, as well as Exiled Force (for monster removal) and Injection Fairy Lily (sheer power).

Des Lacooda ensures that you don't fall too far behind on hand advantage – he works great with Giant Rat. If your opponent attacks Rat with the last monster he has on the field, summon Des Lacooda. You'll be able to flip him face-down via his effect, then Flip Summon him on your next turn, thereby drawing a card. This didn't used to be legal, but now it is.

D.D. Warrior Lady and *D.D. Assailant* are great against Vampire Lord and Sacred Phoenix of Nephthys, since they more or less shut down those monsters' effects.

Spear Dragon's always a nice surprise – a powerful monster with a piercing effect. Great for taking out those Sheep Tokens.

Des Koala is one of the more rentsy monsters in the deck. Almost nobody expects it, and with 1800 DEF, there's a good chance it won't die when your opponent attacks it. There's also a good chance you'll do 1200-1600 damage with Koala alone – not bad at all.

Night Assailant is great for getting back lost Flip Effects,

and in this deck there are a bunch. Similarly, *Tsukuyomi* allows you to reuse those still on the field.

Qualified Spells

The Spells for the most part are self-explanatory, with a few rentsy exceptions. *Messenger of Peace* is great for stalling until you get the cards you need to pound your opponent into the ground.

Wave-Motion Cannon not only may make your opponent nervous; it may also win you the game on its own, if your opponent is unfortunate enough not to draw any Spell or Trap removal.

Book of Moon is the most versatile Spell in the deck. It can reuse your Flip Effects, stop an opponent's monster, make a monster easier to defeat in battle, block against certain Spells and Traps…the list goes on.

The two oddball Traps are Cease-fire, one of my all-time favorite cards; and The Spell Absorbing Life. In addition to doing potentially major damage and/or gaining you potentially major Life Points, these two can save your monsters (especially Guardian Sphinx) from cards like Nobleman of Crossout and stop your opponent's Flip Effects before they start.

This is the kind of deck that'll take your opponent by surprise. It's unpredictable; it's everywhere; it's rentsy.

MONSTER: 18

1x Guardian Sphinx
2x Giant Rat
2x Des Lacooda
1x Exiled Force
1x Injection Fairy Lily
1x D.D. Warrior Lady
1x D.D. Assailant
1x Magician of Faith
1x Morphing Jar
1x Night Assailant
1x Sangan
1x Spear Dragon
1x Breaker the Magical Warrior
1x Cyber Jar
1x Tsukuyomi
1x Des Koala

SPELL: 14

2x Smashing Ground
2x Messenger of Peace
1x Dark Hole
1x Snatch Steal
1x Nobleman of Crossout
1x Heavy Storm
1x Mystical Space Typhoon
1x Swords of Revealing Light
1x Wave-Motion Cannon
1x Premature Burial
1x Book of Moon
1x Lightning Vortex

TRAP: 8

2x Bottomless Trap Hole
1x Dust Tornado
1x Call of the Haunted
1x Ceasefire
1x The Spell Absorbing Life
1x Magic Cylinder
1x Torrential Tribute

Advanced Alchemy Deck
Advanced Format

By: Snapper

Wouldn't you like to know how to do alchemy? You know, turning some useless piece of metal into **gold**? If you would, then you should make an Alchemy Deck!

Better yet, use this guide. Not only will it constantly encourage you to master equivalent exchange, but it will find a use for many forgotten YGO cards, almost all of which are **common.**

Where to Start

To start off, you'll need to look for six Element monsters like *Element Doom* and *Element Magician,* which gain effects from monsters of specific Attributes. Preferably, you'll want to select monsters that gain power from FIRE monsters, seeing as that is the most useful of the effects available (it gives the monster a 500 ATK increase). *Element Dragon* and *Element Saurus* are two such monsters, so we're going to use three of each.

Being an Alchemy Deck, *Homunculus the Alchemic Being **is a necessity.*** And with 1800 ATK and the ability to change its Attribute at will, you're definitely going to want to use three of it.

UFO Turtle, while unconventional, is something that can be very helpful for this Deck. Not only does it allow Deck thinning, but it can also keep Element Dragon and Element Saurus at 2000 ATK even after it's died in battle by summoning other UFO Turtles. And because it works best in threes, we'll use three of these spaceship tortoises.

Elemental Mistress Doriado is next up on our to-add list. Not only does she allow your Element monsters to use both of their effects, but also she single-

Monsters: 18

- 3 - Element Dragon
- 3 - Element Saurus
- 3 - Homunculus the Alchemic Being
- 3 - UFO Turtle
- 2 - Elemental Mistress Doriado
- 2 - Manju of the Ten Thousand Hands
- 1 - Morphing Jar
- 1 - Sangan

Spells: 16

- 2 - Creature Swap
- 2 - Doriado's Blessing
- 2 - Scroll of Bewitchment
- 2 - Smashing Ground
- 1 - Dark Hole
- 1 - Heavy Storm
- 1 - Mystical Space Typhoon
- 1 - Nobleman of Crossout
- 1 - Premature Burial
- 1 - Scapegoat
- 1 - Snatch Steal
- 1 - Swords of Revealing Light

9 ptTraps: 6

- 3 - Fuh-Rin-Ka-Zan
- 1 - Call of the Haunted
- 1 - Ceasefire
- 1 - Torrential Tribute

handedly meets the requirements for Fuh-Rin-Ka-Zan. Of course, she IS a weak Ritual Monster, so we'll only use two of her. We'll add some protection too, just to keep her safe.

If we're going to use Doriado (and her Ritual Spell) we'll need **at least two** Manju of the Ten Thousand Hands. It just makes Ritual Summons that much easier.

Scroll of Bewitchment (a Spell if you've lost track) is something that can assist in acquiring specific Attributes. Because the majority of the monsters do not provide any of the four elements right off the bat, **you'll want** Scroll of Bewitchment **to turn them into an Attribute that can be more useful.** I'll use two, but given the large amounts of Attribute switchers you already have, you may want to use something else.

Finish it Off

The final ingredient needed to make this Alchemy Deck unique is **Fuh-Rin-Ka-Zan, a Trap with FOUR groundbreaking effects** that is easily activated when you have Doriado on the field. So because of our two Doriados and the boatload of Attribute transformers in this Deck, we'll use three.

So now you've got 23 slots of your Deck occupied. Fill the rest with generic *"staples"*, and you get a *"masterpiece"*.

And there you have it; an Alchemy Deck for you personal use that works like second grade clockwork. It's far from making you the next Edward Elric, but it's as

close as you'll get for a long time. So make it, beat the competition with it, work on turning aluminum into gold, and most of all, have fun! May your Duels be happy ones, for you are the Full Throttle Duelist.

31

Suicide Beatdown "Terminal Velocity"
Advanced Format

By: Joseph "Otaku" Lee

Megamorph is an Equip Spell that's effect varies according to the owner's LP. If the owner has *less LP* than the opponent, the base ATK of the equipped Monster is doubled. If owner has *the same LP* as the opponent, there is no effect. Finally, if the owner's LP is higher than the opponent's, the equipped Monster's base ATK is halved. With all those possibilities, there's got to be something fun we can do with it, right?

Strategy

Suicide Beatdown is a deck where you spend your own LP on a variety of effects. Generally, you'll try to frustrate your opponent and peck away at their LP just a hair slower than you spend your own. *After that, wait until you have a safe opening for a direct attack*, drop a *Megamorph* on your best attacker and go for game. Any cards not listed below are ones common to most decks, and need no real explanation.

Monster Cards

Amazoness Swords Woman's effect shifts the battle damage you take to your opponent, but only if she is involved in the battle. Megamorph their biggest Monster and ram her into it. If you don't finish them off, you'll probably have crippled that Monster's ATK score. *Exiled Force* is Monster Removal, though at the cost of a Summon. *Injection Fairy Lily* can become big enough to overwhelm most commonly played Monsters for 2000 LP per battle. *Giant Rat can search out and Special Summon the previous three Monsters if it dies in battle.* Cyber-Stein can Special Summon any of your Fusions. Enraged Battle Ox can still do battle damage when attacking a Monster in DEF position. Jirai Gumo is a large 2200 ATK Level 4 Beatstick that can cost half your LP when it attacks – ideal for this deck.

Spell Cards

Card Destruction is a double-edged sword: it can disrupt the opponent and speed up your deck or theirs. Confiscation not only lets you see the opponent's hand and discard the biggest threat while lowering your LP by a comfortable 1000. Use *Enemy Controller* to clear out weakened Monsters from your own field and borrow an opponent's Monster for a turn. Megamorph is the cornerstone of the deck, but you'll usually use two, tops.

Trap Cards

Ceasefire reveals facedown threats and Magic Cylinder negates a single Monster's attack… and both burn the opponent. Solemn Judgment allows you to reduce your LP while negating your opponent's most important moves – *again, don't expect to use all three most duels.* Activate Royal Decree at the last minute to negate a freshly activate Trap.

Fusion Deck

For the most part, just use whatever you want in here, as there is no limit on how many Fusions you can run. *Cyber End Dragon is definitely a must* though, as it can score a very easy victory – after being Megamorphed, it has 8000 ATK and still does damage against Defense Position Monsters.

Monster Cards x 16 [40 cards]

1 Amazoness Swords Woman
1 Breaker The Magical Warrior MFC-071
1 Cyber Jar MRL-077
1 Cyber-Stein
1 D.D. Warrior Lady
2 Enraged Battle Ox
1 Exiled Force
2 Giant Rat
1 Injection Fair Lily
2 Jirai Gumo
1 Magician of Faith SDJ-017
1 Morphing Jar TP4-002
1 Sangan

Spell Cards x 15

1 Book of Moon
1 Card Destruction
1 Confiscation
1 Dark Hole
2 Enemy Controller
1 Heavy Storm
3 Megamorph
1 Mystical Space Typhoon SYE-037
1 Nobleman of Crossout
1 Premature Burial
1 Smashing Ground
1 Snatch Steal

Trap Cards x 9

3 Solemn Judgment
1 Torrential Tribute LON-25
1 Call of the Haunted
1 Ceasefire PSV-030
1 Dust Tornado
1 Magic Cylinder
1 Royal Decree

Side Deck (15 cards)

2 Return from the Different Dimension
2 King Tiger Wanghu
1 Enraged Battle Ox
1 Enemy Controller
3 Berserk Gorilla
3 Des Wombat
1 Dust Tornado
1 Soul Release

Fusion Deck (4+ cards)

1 Cyber End Dragon
1 Dark Balter the Terrible
1 Ryu Senshi
1 Thousand-Eyes Restrict
? Whatever else you feel like

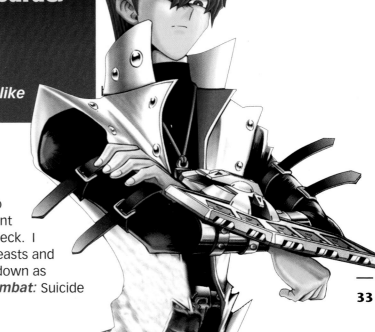

Fusions can only
brought out via Cyber-
in this deck, so don't
to use most of them.

Side Deck

This is the key to this deck is the side deck. Why? This deck is supposed to keeping your opponent guessing. Do not run it week after week. Most of the time, you will want to switch to a second deck type concealed in your Side Deck. I find that a Beastdown deck, that is a deck built around Beasts and Beast-Warriors, a good fit. You can also run Suicide Beatdown as a side deck only strategy. Either way, remember *Des Wombat:* Suicide Beatdown is ***very vulnerable*** to Burn, which it blocks.

33

▶ Decks to Beat - *Killer Decks* ◀◀

Monarch/Soul Control
Advanced Format

By: Samuel Pecharka

Zaborg the Thunder Monarch, Mobius the Frost Monarch, Thestalos the Firestorm Monarch, and Granmarg the Rock Monarch all share the unique classification of being *"monarch"* cards. While they may not be the most supreme Monsters, they certainly made an impression upon the metagame. Some players even elected to create a deck based just upon a combination of these **four phenomenal cards** and exploiting their effects to create a unique and commanding theme.

> All monarchs have statistics of 2400 ATK and 1000 DEF making them one-Tribute monstrosities.

About Monarchs

All monarchs have statistics of 2400 ATK and 1000 DEF, making them **one-Tribute monstrosities.** The 1000 DEF makes monarchs susceptible to Tsukuyomi, a minor flaw in their composition. The monarchs' effects trigger in the same way: en-Tribute Summon. Each monarch represents a separate Attribute, though there are no DARK or WIND monarchs. **Only Zaborg is able to be morphed into Dark Balter the Terrible;** the rest have six stars. As you can see, these cards are annoyingly similar. However, that does not mean that there are not superior and inferior monarchs; quite the opposite: only two of them are even worth playing in a competitive deck.

18 Monsters:

2 Mobius the Frost Monarch
3 Thestalos the Firestorm Monarch
3 Berserk Gorilla
2 D. D. Assailant
1 Breaker the Magical Warrior
1 D. D. Warrior Lady
2 Gravekeeper's Spy
1 Tsukuyomi
1 Sangan
1 Morphing Jar
1 Spirit Reaper

15 Spells:

2 Different Dimension Capsule
1 Confiscation
1 Dark Hole
1 Nobleman of Crossout
1 Book of Moon
1 Heavy Storm
1 Mystical Space Typhoon
1 Premature Burial
1 Snatch Steal
1 Brain Control
2 Soul Exchange
1 Swords of Revealing Light
1 Scapegoat

7 Traps:

1 Bottomless Trap Hole
1 Call of the Haunted
3 Sakuretsu Armor
1 Torrential Tribute
1 Ceasefire

Zaborg the Thunder Monarch and Granmarg the Rock Monarch, while retaining versatility and destructiveness, have the nasty ability to affect the user as well as his or her opponent. This is because their effects are **mandatory**, whereas Mobius the Frost Monarch's effect is **optional** and Thestalos the Firestorm Monarch's effect is **not applicable.** If you Tribute Summon Zaborg or Granmarg and your opponent does not have a monster or face-down card to destroy, you must destroy one of your own, respectively. (Granmarg can get around this because having Granmarg on the field need not mandate you to have a face-down card as well; Zaborg, on the other hand, will automatically destroy itself if you have no other monsters.)

Other Problems

There are other issues affecting **Zaborg the Thunder Monarch and Granmarg the Rock Monarch.** These two monsters **do not fit with the other monarch cards** such that they are incapable of feeding off each others' strengths and weaknesses. **Mobius the Frost Monarch and Thestalos the Firestorm Monarch,** however, compliment each other by providing a sure advantage, regardless of whichever one of them is summoned (that is to say, they are synergetic to one another). In addition, Mobius the Frost Monarch directly provides *"card advantage"* through its effect, a scant ability in the Pot of Greed-ridden metagame of today.

Monarch decks are able to compete well because they can **manipulate the dueling conditions** with ease. Whereas many other decks struggle to gain field or hand presence, in an instant, a Monarch deck can alter the field or hand such that they gain a commanding lead. Soul Control pioneer *Evan Vargas* impressively piloted a variation of a Monarch deck to the top eight of a **Shonen Jump Championship.** Countless others qualified and used Monarch decks at even larger tournaments, like the **United States National Championship.** Obviously, the Monarch deck is one to behold.

35

Lava Lockdown
Advanced Format

By: Mike "Dawn Yoshi" Rosenberg

Since its release, I've found Lava Golem to be one of the most intriguing monsters ever. Its use can justify your uttering of the phrase, *"Gosh, I love burning things"*, in public!

Okay, so maybe nothing can justify uttering that phrase ever. However, Lava Golem is easily one of the **best monsters to run in a burner/stall deck,** and Lava Lockdown is made to abuse Lava Golem as much as possible. The greatest strength of Lava Golem is that **the monsters you tribute from your opponent's field cannot be saved, as sacrificing those monsters is a cost to special summon Lava Golem.** This means that even if your opponent negates Lava Golem's summon, they will still lose

their monsters. The opponent may even be tempted to waste cards on removing Lava Golem from the field in order to keep the behemoth from winning you the duel. This puts a great deal of psychological pressure on your opponent, and it will force them to make decisions that will **always leave them with a disadvantage.** After all, they can either suffer damage each turn the behemoth is face-up on their field, or they can lose a good deal of cards just to prevent its effect!

Zero Out Your Opponent

Stealth Bird and *Cannon Soldier* both aid in reducing the opponent's life points to zero through card effects, which is the win condition for the Lava Lockdown deck. *Des Lacooda*

Monsters: 17

Lava Golem x3
Stealth Bird x3
Des Lacooda x3
Mask of Darkness x2
Magician of Faith
Sangan
Spirit Reaper x2
Cannon Soldier
Breaker the Magical Warrior

Spells: 12

Dark Hole
Swords of Revealing Light
Mystical Space Typhoon
Snatch Steal
Giant Trunade
Messenger of Peace x2
Book of Moon
Level Limit – Area B x2
Wave-Motion Cannon x2

Traps: 11

Solemn Judgment x3
Ojama Trio x3
Gravity Bind
Call of the Haunted
Compulsory Evacuation Device x2
Torrential Tribute

is the draw engine of this deck, as it benefits from the variety of stall you are running in your spell and trap line-up, and it allows you to draw into your counter traps and win conditions a lot faster. If you manage to start flip summoning two Des Lacoodas each turn, it's safe to say that you will win the duel. The rest of the monsters are pretty self-explanatory, as *Spirit Reaper* aids in stalling the opponent's attacks, Mask of Darkness returns essential trap cards from your graveyard, *Sangan* is a powerful search effect, and *Breaker the Magical Warrior* is always ridiculously powerful.

Spells and Traps

The spell and trap line-up for Lava Lockdown is specifically focused on holding off the opponent's attacks. It is **crucial** that you keep your attack-prevention continuous spells active throughout your duels, as your monsters will not survive battle. You probably wouldn't like having the Lava Golem that you gave the opponent smashing you with fiery fury each turn either. The most notable trap card that does not aid the stall strategy, however, is Ojama Trio. This card can help you reduce your opponent's life points to zero, but it serves the role of disrupting your opponent's ability to summon monsters. More importantly, ***two activations of Ojama Trio usually locks down your opponent's***

monster zone, which will allow you to win through your burn effects. You can also tribute off Ojama tokens in order to special summon Lava Golem!

Explore the joys of summoning fiery titans for your opponent! You may see that, with a proper side deck, that Lava Lockdown can be one of the best decks in this advanced format.

37

▲▲ Decks to Beat - *Killer Decks* ◄◄

Clown Control 2.0
Advanced Format

By: Mike "Dawn Yoshi" Rosenberg

Many years ago, duelists existed in the dark age of Yu-Gi-Oh, where every deck was forced to conform to running nothing but a bunch of big bruisers. The goal of each deck was to bludgeon the opponent's life points with as many big bad attacks as possible. This made some duelists sad. However, in the midst of the dark ages, **the wonders of stall were released** from the **Pharaoh's Servant** booster set! This made those sad duelists very happy, as it gave them the opportunity to destroy their opponents with… clowns?! Yeah, that's right. **Clowns!**

Clown Control was one of the first successful control decks in Yu-Gi-Oh, as the deck theme utilized the elements of **Dream Clown and Crass Clown** to control the opponent's monster zone. The Clown Control duelist could then use cards like **Hayabusa Knight** to reduce the opponent's life points to zero.

That was Then

Times have changed, and many new control decks have been created, tested, and played successfully in major tournaments. However, with the rise of the new advanced format, Clown Control has been given a second chance to shine! **The basic strategy of Clown Control 2.0 is the same as the original Clown Control deck.** Your goal is to control the opponent's monster zone with Dream Clown, with the aid of other control monsters and your stall spells. You can then swing for the win with **Horus the Black Flame Dragon LV6,** which is unaffected by all of your stall elements. Dream Clown is easily the most versatile control monster because it can be summoned to the field quickly. You can naturally draw and summon Dream Clown, fetch it to your hand with **Reinforcement of the Army,** or you can special summon it

Monsters: 17

Dream Clown x3
Horus the Black Flame Dragon LV6 x2
Giant Rat x3
Des Lacooda x2
Golem Sentry
Exiled Force
Big Shield Gardna
Sangan
Medusa Worm
Magician of Faith
Breaker the Magical Warrior

Spells: 17

Dark Hole
Swords of Revealing Light
Heavy Storm
Mystical Space Typhoon
Snatch Steal
Premature Burial
Level Limit – Area B x2
Messenger of Peace x3
Book of Moon
Stumbling x3
Giant Trunade
Reinforcement of the Army

Traps: 6

Solemn Judgment x3
Spiritual Earth Art – Kurogane
Call of the Haunted
Torrential Tribute

during the damage step with *Giant Rat!*

Speaking of Giant Rat, this earth attribute fetch-monster has the ability to special summon far more than Dream Clown. For example, if you are running low on resources, it may be better to special summon *Des Lacooda,* which can reward you with an amazingly large amount of card advantage. You could also special summon *Golem Sentry,* which is the ultimate weapon in dealing with *The Sacred Phoenix of Nephthys. Exiled Force* **and** *Big Shield Gardna* are also possible targets for Giant Rat's effect, and they can be fetched to your hand via Reinforcement of the Army.

Clown Power

The most powerful spell card in Clown Control 2.0 is *Stumbling*. This amazing continuous spell not only disrupts the opponent's tempo in attacking, but it immediately triggers Dream Clown's effect when you summon the little warrior. This means that you will be able to destroy a monster *as soon as Dream Clown is summoned to the field,* whether it's through a normal summon or through Giant Rat's special summon during your opponent's battle phase! The rest of the spell cards in this deck either possess an element of stall or removal, while the trap cards aid in monster recursion, monster removal, and negation.

Dream Clown is still one of the most powerful and versatile control monsters in this game. That fact is confirmed with Clown Control 2.0, a deck which has gained popularity among a few duelists in this new format. Don't fear the reaper. Fear the clown instead!

Tomato Control
Advanced Format

By: Michael Lucas

Decks don't need super-powerful monsters to win. It's entirely possible to go through a Duel (and win) without *ever* having a monster with over 2,400 ATK points hit the field, and have the majority of your monsters be *well under 2,000 ATK.* Effect monsters rule all now! And with so many of these great monsters being searchable by *Mystic Tomato,* Mystic Tomato and his friends are a great deck idea to focus on.

Monsters

Mystic Tomato is obviously the core card of the deck; when he's destroyed in battle, he can search out *Don Zaloog, Newdoria, Sangan,* or *Spirit Reaper.* Don Zaloog and Spirit Reaper can provide hand discarding; Reaper also serves as a defensive wall if switched to Defense Position next turn. Newdoria can dispatch any opponent's monster when it's destroyed in battle, and Sangan can net you an extra card in hand when he's destroyed – all great effects. *Exiled Force, Morphing Jar,* and *D. D. Warrior Lady* can all be searched with *Sangan* and either get rid of opposing monsters or opposing hand advantage. The *D. D. Assailants* and *Breaker the Magical Warrior* are too good to pass up with their respective removal effects, and finally, *Mobius the Frost Monarch* is the tribute monster of choice as he not only provides great advantage by destroying 2

Monsters: 18

3 Mystic Tomato
2 Spirit Reaper
2 Newdoria
2 Don Zaloog
1 Sangan
1 Breaker the Magical Warrior
1 Exiled Force
1 Morphing Jar
2 D. D. Assailant
1 D. D. Warrior Lady
2 Mobius the Frost Monarch

Spells: 15

2 Reinforcements of the Army
1 Heavy Storm
1 Mystical Space Typhoon
1 Dark Hole
2 Smashing Ground
1 Nobleman of Crossout
1 Book of Moon
1 Messenger of Peace
1 Swords of Revealing Light
1 Scapegoat
1 Premature Burial
1 Snatch Steal
1 Wave-Motion Cannon

Traps: 7

2 Sakuretsu Armor
1 Mirror Wall
2 Dust Tornado
1 Call of the Haunted
1 Torrential Tribute

opposing spell or trap cards, but with so many searches coming from Tomatoes, it won't be that hard to bring him out.

Spells

Reinforcement of the Army provides an alternate path to your D. D. Assailants and Warrior Lady, along with Don Zaloog and Exiled Force. Heavy Storm, Dark Hole, and Mystical Space Typhoon are necessary additions to almost any deck and this is no exception; the massive destruction of all types of cards is just too good to overlook. Smashing Grounds get rid of opposing monsters that your monsters can't handle; Nobleman of Crossout can stop a particularly nasty effect from going off from a face-down. Book of Moon, Swords of Revealing Light, Scapegoat, and Messenger of Peace can protect you for many turns. Premature and Snatch belong in all decks for the revival and monster theft. *Wave-Motion Cannon is a great little addition to this deck* – the opponent will most

likely waste all their spell and trap removal on your powerful traps and extra stalling spell cards, so once they've used it up, or if you can't seem to break through to their life points, this card gives you an alternate way to win the game.

Traps

Sakuretsu Armors take care of big threats; Dust Tornado clears out opposing Spell/Traps so your weenies can rush for quick hits, and Call and Torrential, like Premature and Snatch, should be automatic inclusions. *Mirror Wall is the one that needs explaining* – this card combos with Don Zaloog to turn an opponent's attack into a lost monster and a lost card in hand.

To sum it all up, this deck has many ways of either providing field and hand advantage to its player or depriving the same

from an opponent. This is what the new format is all about, so the deck deserves a try. Run it yourself and see if it works for you!

▶▶ Decks to Beat - *Killer Decks* ◀◀

Camel Control
Advanced Format

By: Michael Lucas

The most important things in the current Advanced format are **hand advantage and controlling the field.** It doesn't take a Warrior Toolbox deck full of super-strong monsters to hold down the field; rather, sometimes it's good to have weaker monsters, depending on the Spell and Trap cards you play. The following deck focuses on *Des Lacooda,* who with the right protection, can be a power-house of card-drawing – and the cards you draw can only further help the stalling and burning you'll be doing. Here's the prototype decklist, thanks to {//[RU1]\\} from the *Pojo.biz* forums, who engineered the idea:

Monsters:

This deck ***doesn't play completely*** like a normal stall/burn. Sure, the Stealth Birds are there for flipping face-up then back face-down for 1,000 damage, but that's where the similarities end. **Des Lacooda is the star of the deck,** earning you card advantage for stalling – 1 card per turn to be exact, for when you Flip Summon him and then return him F/D. ***Against a locked field,*** *Swarm of Scarabs/Locusts are great;* they can pick off opposing monsters and

42

Monsters: 16

3 Des Lacooda
3 Mystic Tomato
2 Swarm of Scarabs
2 Swarm of Locusts
3 Stealth Bird
2 Spirit Reaper
1 Sangan

Spells: 12

3 Messenger of Peace
2 Level Limit – Area B
1 Swords of Revealing Light
1 Mystical Space Typhoon
3 Wave-Motion Cannon
1 Premature Burial
1 Book of Moon

Traps: 12

3 Sakuretsu Armor
3 Solemn Judgment
2 Gravity Bind
2 Spell Shield – Type 8
1 Dust Tornado
1 Ceasefire

spell/trap cards, possibly get small hits in, and then flip down to do it again. ***Reapers are the best of monster defense.*** *Mystic Tomato* can search any monster in the deck except for Des Lacooda. ***Finally, Sangan can search any monster in the deck period!*** Now THAT'S a true toolbox of a searcher!

Spells:

The philosophy is stall, stall, stall some more, and burn in the spells department. Messenger of Peace doesn't hinder any of your monsters; Level Limit only stops your Tomatoes from attacking. Swords serves to further block attacks. Mystical Space Typhoon picks off a possible opposing Dust Tornado before it can be used; Premature makes the cut to revive another monster (who, if it flips itself face-down, gets rid of the hindrance of being equipped with it), and Book of Moon serves as an additional attack-block or flip-helper. The best part has to be the 3 Wave-Motion Cannons though – letting these charge for a few turns will make an opponent panic, scrambling to get rid of them however possible. But even if the opponent has spell/trap removal, it ***doesn't*** mean it's going to work…

Traps:

…because there's more than enough in here to stop those. Solemn Judgments are there just for that purpose. Spell Shields not only stop Noblemans and some quick-play spells, but can be used as Magic Jammers as well. With Des Lacooda giving extra draws, suddenly that becomes viable! Gravity Bind serves to lock the field and Sakuretsu Armors destroy what does get through. Dust Tornado picks off a spell/trap before it can be chained, and ***Ceasefire can be the last bit of burn needed to win a Duel.***

This is a great deck for those who want to try dominating with something new, and it really is a solid build a skilled player should feel confident taking into a tournament. Who knows – we might all be net-decking this in the near future. As I recommend with all Killer Decks I write about, the best way to find out is to make the deck yourself, so get out there and do it!

◄◄ Decks to Beat - *Killer Decks* ►►

RelinquisH YouR ControL
Advanced Format

By: Coin Flip

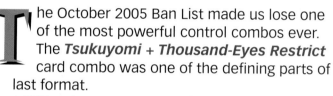

BOTTOMLESS TRAP HOLE 罠
[TRAP CARD]

When your opponent Normal Summons, Flip Summons, or Special Summons a monster, a monster with an ATK of 1500 or more, the monster is destroyed and removed from play.

The October 2005 Ban List made us lose one of the most powerful control combos ever. The ***Tsukuyomi + Thousand-Eyes Restrict*** card combo was one of the defining parts of last format.

Without easy access to Thousand-Eyes Restrict, as well as being limited to only one copy of the powerful fusion monster, the combo has been dismantled. However, here's a thought: ***Why not use the better half of Restrict's Fusion Material Monsters?*** Today you get to see one of my pet decks. I present to you ***"RelinquisH YouR ControL"***!

Monster Speed

The Monster section is focused on intense speed. ***Relinquished and Chaos Sorcerer are both Special Summons,*** allowing you to tribute them to Mobius the Frost Monarch to gain card advantage and clear the field of your opponent's threats. The last three monsters are arguably staple monsters, and Tsukuyomi allows you to reuse the effect of Relinquished, Chaos Sorcerer, Magician of Faith, Magical Merchant AND Manju of the Ten Thousand Hands! Simply incredible!

The Spells section is very barebones. I don't make extravagant lineups here because I want heavy trap

protection. This deck lacks field presence. The Traps take care of that.

Whoah, whoah! That's a lot of Traps! But wait. ***The deck is reliant upon keeping itself alive while gaining card advantage.*** Card advantage is nothing if they have too many cards. All the 1 for 1's in here intensify the strength of the card advantage engines such as Chaos Sorcerer and Relinquished. ***Call of the Haunted and Torrential Tribute*** are simply solid cards.

Fuse Up Your Fusions

The next thing to consider here is the Fusion Deck. Obviously, you want one Thousand-Eyes

44

Monsters: 16

- 3x *Manju of the Ten Thousand Hands*
- 3x *Relinquished*
- 2x *Chaos Sorcerer*
- 2x *Mobius the Frost Monarch*
- 1x *Magician of Faith*
- 1x *Magical Merchant*
- 1x *Tsukuyomi*
- 1x *Sangan*
- 1x *Breaker the Magical Warrior*
- 1x *D. D. Warrior Lady*

Spells: 14

- 3x *Black Illusion Ritual*
- 1x *Dark Hole*
- 1x *Heavy Storm*
- 1x *Snatch Steal*
- 1x *Brain Control*
- 1x *Premature Burial*
- 1x *Mystical Space Typhoon*
- 1x *Nobleman of Crossout*
- 1x *Swords of Revealing Light*
- 1x *Book of Moon*
- 1x *Scapegoat*
- 1x *Metamorphosis*

Traps: 11

- 3x *Sakuretsu Armor*
- 3x *Dust Tornado*
- 2x *Bottomless Trap Hole*
- 1x *Call of the Haunted*
- 1x *Torrential Tribute*

Fusions: 4

- 1x *Thousand-Eyes Restrict*
- 2x *Ryu Senshi*
- 1x *Dark Blade the Dragon Knight*

Side Deck: 15

- 3x *Spirit Reaper*
- 3x *Gravekeeper's Spy*
- 3x *Solemn Judgment*
- 3x *Threatening Roar*
- 3x *Elephant Statue of Disaster*

Restrict in there… But why not a *Ryu Senshi* as well, in case you ever want to morph a Chaos Sorcerer into another monster? A *Dark Blade the Dragon Knight* wouldn't be a bad idea either.

On the Side

The last thing to consider is our *Side Deck*. While most decks won't be too big of a problem do to the universal monster removal of Relinquished and s/t removal of Dust Tornado and Mobius, some decks will be annoying to face. Burn will clog your field up with Ojama Trio and then tribute your monsters to Lava Golem, ruining your setup. *The counter:* add hand control that slips underneath annoying cards like Gravity Bind. So we'll add in three Spirit Reapers (which also helps against Exodia). If you go up against beatdown, some field presence would be nice, so we'll add Gravekeeper's Spies, which have 2000 DEF and search another GK Spy out in defense position when flipped face-up.

Solemn Judgments are good against any deck, and three copies of Elephant Statue of Disaster will help against Last Turn. Finally, three copies of Threatening Roar for Ben Kai decks.

◀ Decks to Beat - Killer Decks ◀◀

The Black Flame Dragon

Advanced Format

By: Darrel Dorigatti
a.k.a. "Leon"

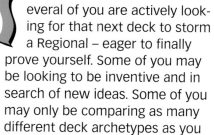

Several of you are actively looking for that next deck to storm a Regional – eager to finally prove yourself. Some of you may be looking to be inventive and in search of new ideas. Some of you may only be comparing as many different deck archetypes as you can in search of that one concept that can truly be called the best.

Regardless of your intentions I hope to teach you all a little lesson. The best deck out there is whatever deck you decide to make. The deck that will be the most successful to you is the one you are most comfortable with.

Synergy, Consistency, Control, Power: These are terms we may use to describe how to make a deck the best it can be, but they are not the most important things to remember. Most important of all is a player's **skill and comfort level** with the deck they have chosen to construct.

You should not have to adapt to the deck. Make the deck adapt to you.

I am going to lay this deck in front of you, but instead of describing things traditionally I want you all to see how it came to be constructed. We are going to take an analytical approach from start to finish. I want you to take the mental journey with me; think as I do. I do this in hopes that one day, when you are finally in the mood to go for something new, you can use my advice to figure out how

46

best to make a deck work for you.

The first step in the construction of any deck should be to **pick a goal** (we also call this a *theme*). What is your win condition? What combos or concepts do you want your deck to exploit? You can use more than one, but to maintain consistency (and prevent a problem commonly seen among newer players) I want you to pick only 2 or 3 choices maximum.

You guys with me so far? Good. Following the first step, I will ask myself the question, **"What do I want to do?"** Well, I notice that often times my opponent's spell and trap cards really get in my way. I just want to be able to attack and not worry about any of that stuff. So it seems I can have two clear goals from that statement:

1. *To shut down my opponent's Spell Cards.*
2. *To shut down my opponent's Trap Cards.*

I can stick with these, because experience has given me a good idea of how to approach the theme. With these two goals one should also make a third, implied goal. That goal should be **to use the advantage obtained to capitalize and defeat my opponent.**

I have my goals. What should I do next? Once you have these goals firmly set you need to do research to figure out which cards are needed to do achieve the desired result. Specifically, I need to research and find card(s) that can shut down my opponent's traps and shut down my opponent's spells. Often times

you have a good idea of the cards to use. Other times you're more clueless. In following this step I have chosen to use two cards:

1. *Horus the Black Flame Dragon LV8 - This card cannot be Normal Summoned or Set. This card cannot be Special Summoned except by the effect of "Horus the Black Flame Dragon LV6". As long as this card remains face-up on your side of the field, you can negate the activation and effect of any Spell Cards and destroy them.*
2. *Royal Decree - As long as this card remains face-up on the field, negate the effects of all Trap Cards on the field except this card.*

For obvious reasons, just by reading these effects, you should know that they are worthy choices. Be careful though, because this may not always be the case. Effects may not be so direct but due to other factors such as card rulings, errata, or unique combinations with other cards they may end up being the best choice for your goal.

With the identification of the actual cards to use you have taken a deck idea (a mere concept) and transformed it into a deck core (something tangible and producible). The core of the deck should be the constant: **the physical manifestation of the initial goal** you and your deck are trying to achieve. What next?

Well…everything else is just building around it.

It takes some work, but there are many people more willing to help you when you have already reached this step. This is the step where the term *"support"* comes in. The bulk of the cards in your deck should have this role. It's an important concept and something that newer players often times overlook. It is always better to have a deck with a few goals and lots of support dedicated to it, than to have a deck with many different goals and combos, and a sequential lack of support for them.

Getting Started

Let's start seeing what we actually need. For Horus LV8 to get its effect it first needs to be summoned to the field. That should be a big clue to some of its support. **We need *Horus LV6* to be summoned to the field first** and, as a tribute monster, may require an additional amount of support to become easier to manage. Cards such as Snatch Steal and Brain Control allow a player to take control of a face up monster and

47

use it as they see fit. It's a solid choice for a direct line of support as often times you would much rather want to tribute your opponent's monster instead of your own. Monsters that can maintain, or even increase, their field presence are also good choices, as the chance of you being able to tribute summon later on becomes greater. *Royal Decree does not require as much direct support to use successfully,* but the key thing to remember about this card is written into its own effect. Royal Decree negates all traps when on the field - *not just the opponents.* We need to make sure we are not locking down too much of our own cards as well, so we will attempt to keep the trap line up at a strictly basic line of defense.

The Support

Here's a list of cards in this deck that provide primary support for the management and eventual abuse of Horus LV6 and LV8: Nimble Momonga, Giant Rat, Snatch Steal, Brain Control, Level Up!, Premature Burial, and Call of the Haunted. As primary support these cards help give you what you really need in order to run a deck with three tribute monsters successfully.

Next we have what I call *secondary support,* or "filler". It is much harder to get a solid definition of this type of support, but

there are many ways to find good secondary support cards. An easy way to do this would be to ask a series of questions:

What can my opponent do to stop my theme/deck/combo?

What ways could I deal with or prevent these tactics?

What would be the best choice?

I have chosen to include a commonly seen line of cards based on this series of questioning: Solemn Judgment, Confiscation, Messenger of Peace, Nobleman of Crossout, Smashing Ground, Dark Hole, Heavy Storm, Mystical Space Typhoon, Exiled Force, Torrential Tribute, and Mystic Swordsman LV2. This list can be read and recognized as being good choices overall, but it is still important that we see why. These cards are designed to *eliminate or prevent those threats most commonly seen to your deck's strategy.* The best way to know what that really includes is it to ask the above questions and actively seek the answers through play-testing.

For example, with both my opponent's spell and trap cards completely locked down what does that leave to still save him? Monsters. And I'm willing to bet that there is a monster out there that can do just that. Not to name any names but most likely it would have the initials *"D.D."* somewhere in there.

That is one of the threats a secondary line-up would then try to eliminate or prevent.

The other main type of secondary support would be what people

Monsters

2x D.D. Assailant
3x Nimble Momonga
3x Berserk Gorilla
2x Giant Rat
Horus the Black Flame Dragon Lv 8
3x Horus the Black Flame Dragon Lv 6
Mystic Swordsman Lv2
Exiled Force
Des Lacooda
Magician of Faith

Spells

Dark Hole
Confiscation
Snatch Steal
Heavy Storm
Mystical Space Typhoon
Premature Burial
Brain Control
2x Smashing Ground
Nobleman of Crossout
2x Creature Swap
Scapegoat
Level Up!
2x Messenger of Peace

Traps

2x Royal Decree
2x Solemn Judgement
Call of the Haunted
Torrential Tribute

Side Deck:

2x Mobius the Frost Monarch
Medusa Worm
2x Muka Muka
2x Dust Tornado
Lightning Vortex
Injection Fairy Lily
Giant Rat
2x Kinetic Soldier
Wave Motion Cannon
2x Sakuretsu Armor

call your *"combo cards."* These cards are generally short, one-two combos that can help either establish advantage, disrupt the opponent, or do both. The most important thing to remember

though is this: *They need to be short and simple.* No complex, situational garbage that you saw Yugi do on TV will really fly.

For example, I activate *Creature Swap* and give you my *Giant Rat.* I attack it and get another creature on my side of the field for more advantage.

Meanwhile, I disrupted you by stealing your monster. It only took two cards, and I could have even

use a *Nimble Momonga* or something else instead. Just keep these combos small.

I know the article has been long, but we have made tremendous progress. I now feel I have given you the basis to begin constructing your own unique works of art. Now I feel confident in showing you the deck list; knowing you guys understand the steps taken to get this far.

You now have the deck. The cards and the concepts are laid in front of you.

Now What?

What should you do next? A crucial thing to remember is that no matter how good you think the deck may be, no matter how confident you are in its success, it is still only a rough draft. The deck is unrefined and not finalized. *Be open to adaptation.*

Play-test: over and over and over again. Make the fixes you feel the deck needs and then play-test some more.

This deck and its analysis were no doubt written differently then some of the other *"Killer Deck ideas"* you may have read in this book. That is only because I wished to teach you something different. Don't just take in all the ideas others throw at you. Find out exactly how they do it and then get creating for yourselves.

And don't tell me there are not any good ideas left! As I write this I can think of ten more decks I have been dieing to try – complete with my own unique spin on all of them. *Just get creating!* Pull out the shoebox and see what you can do.

49

▶▶ Card Strategy ◀◀

The Many Worlds of Yu-Gi-Oh!

By: Michael Lucas

Yu-Gi-Oh! caters to all kinds of people. For some, Yu-Gi-Oh! may just be something a few friends meet up to play after school. Others may play to determine who the best in their small neighborhood is. Some people play, collect, and trade it to the point where they can make a **living** off of it. No matter how old you are, how skilled you are, or how long you've been at it, there's some form of Yu-Gi-Oh that will fit into **your** life best.

Casual Play:

This is how most players started out. Two brothers may have seen the starter decks in the store and have wanted to play just like Yugi does on the cartoon. An anime fan who's followed the Japanese form of the game might want to clash with a few of his friends every so often. The great thing about playing casually is that **anyone can do it,** and it's the most low-pressure environment that exists. Two friends playing at lunch, during recess, or at one another's house most likely won't care if a card was accidentally flipped up or if someone didn't immediately respond to a card played and only remembered they had it later on. It's nearly impossible to start out *"blind"* (immediately starting in tournaments without any previous

good idea to spend a couple of weeks playing and gaining a grasp on the rules here. But once you've done that, it's time to move onto…

League Play:

For almost all players, the weekend Yu-Gi-Oh! League is the first time a player is exposed to other players they don't know, coming together to Duel. Several stores run Yu-Gi-Oh! Leagues on the weekends – *Toys R Us, Books-A-Million,* and some *Wal-Marts* have done so in the past as well. Like playing casually, there's not much pressure or many heated exchanged of words here – so you're not going to get thrown out of league just for trying to *Trap Hole* a *Jinzo* or giving *Breaker the Magical Warrior* a Spell Counter if he's flip-summoned. The

main difference between playing at a League and playing at home is that most likely, someone who is an expert on the game's rules and mechanics will be there to teach you what can and can't be done with certain cards. This is also the first time you'll have a chance to *win prizes,* in the form of promotional cards given out once you accomplish certain things.

However, there are a couple of downsides to Yu-Gi-Oh! Leagues that a player should watch out for – and the stores that do these things should be avoided. Some Leagues set a *maximum age* for their players. Whereas this may seem like an intelligent idea at first, to try to stop older players from possibly taking away

from the experience the younger players would get, the older players are usually the ones that can best help the rest of the league. They have the experience in playing elsewhere, the contact with other players outside of that league, letting them know first-hand what cards work well and which ones don't and can pass that information along to aspiring Duelists. Not allowing older players in a Yu-Gi-Oh! League ends up being *detrimental to every other player there,* who would most likely become better players with the older duelist there to advise them. Additionally, some League stores *disallow trading entirely.* Why go to a league for a trading card game when you can't trade? This hurts all players involved, as people who need specific cards for their deck who would otherwise be able to trade for them can't get them. Before deciding

which local League to attend, I highly recommend speaking with the store manager and finding out their policies.

Once you've taken the advice of the veterans of your local League, and traded for the cards you need to make your deck stronger, it's time to take on…

The Local Tournament:

For new players, this is the **biggest** test of skill they'll have up to this point; for the veterans of the game, it's a chance to test out a **new deck idea** or make their current build stronger. Either way, a player attending an actual sanctioned tournament should know the basic rules, along with any tricky situations that might come up with cards they play. (For example, if you play Last Turn, you should bring out a printout of the rulings for Last Turn from *www.yugioh-card.com* so that

other players can be assured you are using the card correctly.) Tournament play offers the new player a healthy dose of competition – **it's not overwhelming,** like a regional tournament can be, but the player knows he's playing to prove himself, to be the best player of the local crowd, and for whatever prize the tournament organizer or store owner has set aside for the winner. If you're not ready to play in a local tournament, it might be a good idea just to go to one to **watch and talk** to the other players. Oftentimes they're more than happy to help a newcomer figure out how to make their deck better. After a player has a few tournament wins under their belt, and is confident in their deck and playing abilities, it's time to take the next step up, to…

Regional Tournaments and Shonen Jump Championships:

These **huge** events are a challenge for even the long-time players of the game. Regionals tend to have between 100 and 200 players, and **Shonen Jump Championships** usually double that. These events are not for the impatient; these are usually all-day affairs. The other thing to keep in mind is that every player plays every round here – unlike the local tournament, which is usually one loss and you're out, these are run in *Swiss Format* – everyone plays someone who has the same number of wins and losses as they do, and after so many rounds, the top 8 players advance into the final rounds. These final rounds are important, as the top 4 players from each Regional event and the top 8 from a Shonen Jump Championship receive an invite to attend the next **National Championship,** where the best players in the country gather to compete, along with prizes that

can be valued at a few thousand dollars! (The big money prizes are usually only offered to the winner of a Shonen Jump Championship.)

If it's your first time at a Regional or SJC, there are a few things that are very important to remember. First, if you and your opponent have a disagreement on how certain cards work, don't be afraid to call a judge. **The judges are there to help players resolve disputes** and to make sure the day goes smoothly. Additionally, just because you lose a match **does not** mean you're out of the tournament. It's still possible to be one of the top 8 players, even with 2 match losses sometimes. Finally, if you win a match, make sure to take up the slip saying so yourself. Although most players come to a Regional event with only thoughts of honest and fair play, some people might take advantage of a slip left behind, marking themselves as the winner when they actually lost. It's best to make sure situa-

tions like this never occur, so do your part!

If you were skilled enough and lucky enough to acquire an invite, you're only two tournaments away from being the best duelist in the world!

The National and World Championships:

These are the only **two** types of tournaments that require an **invitation** to play in. (The top 100 players in the United States, based on rankings in previous tournaments, may also be allowed to compete in the U.S. Nationals without an invitation.) These tournaments are run just like Regionals, except the stakes are a lot higher. The top 4 players at this event **win a trip to Tokyo, Japan** to com-

pete in the World Championships, where players from every country across the world will compete to see who the absolute **best** Yu-Gi-Oh player is.

The National Championship is most likely the biggest Yu-Gi-Oh TCG experience any of us will ever have, and as such, any duelist attending needs to be in top form. The judging would be more strict here than anywhere else, as all the players involved would be expected to know what cards do and how to deal with issues that came up. However, if you've played well enough to get to this point, you most likely know these things by heart. So at this point, all you can do is trust in your deck, play your best, and do your country proud!

Under The Rose: Online Dueling

By: WiCkEd

Besides playing Yu-Gi-Oh! with paper cards, you can play Yu-Gi-Oh! a variety of ways with friends all over the world. Online Dueling is quite popular, and there are varying ways of doing it. Here's my take on 4 popular methods for dueling online. (Remember, these are simply my thoughts on various programs, your thoughts might vary).

YVD (Yu-Gi-Oh Virtual Desktop) - Or to Some, Online Duelist's Greatest Asset

YVD is an online version of the familiar trading card game, designed for the PC, using the machine to calculate odds, card draws, combat results, etc. Personally, I don't really care for YVD. YVD to me is really only good for deck testing. Why exactly do I dislike YVD?

A.) Shuffle Issues

Mainly when the program shuffles, it shuffles the most broken hand to either you or your opponent and leaves the other player with a horrid hand. I've tried this plenty of times, and 9 times out of 10 it is a major issue.

B.) Finding Cards and Building Decks

Of course, then you have the trouble of actually going though the card database and finding your cards...various cards shown in various rarity forms pollute the whole speed of putting the deck together. One rarity for the same card is fine, no one cares as long as they're dueling.

C.) Inaccuracy of Card Stats

Yeah yeah yeah, so I've had a FEW troubles with this. I basically can let this slide mainly since most people know the stats of cards and such. The

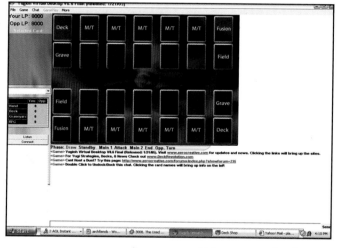

only reason it bugs me is the fact that newbie players get mislead.

D.) Downloading Picture Patches

So this really isn't a big deal overall either. But some people do care. I personally enjoy looking at pictures but it sure as heck isn't high on my "to do" list. But, it is annoying to have such trouble. Hopefully the YVD creators will eventually fix this.

CONCLUSION ON YVD

Do I personally like YVD? No. But, despite its faults it does

have perks, and I mean this in earnest. It's obviously how Max Suffridge worked his way up to the top ranks of the American Duelists. He won Nationals last year. He used YVD constantly. Go Max. YVD is totally how you see it in itself. You either like it or dislike it. You know my opinion, you may have another.

Online Duelist Rating: 5/10 (pending interpretation, its 50/50)

Quality (without pictures): 6/10

Quality (with pictures): 7/10

Overall: It's O.K..

Hm....what's next?

Text Dueling - Or The Less Truthful Choice of All Time

Typical example of an online text duel.

WiCkEd: *Set 1 m.t (Magic or Trap) and end.*

ImginaryD00d: *Set 1 monster and play Nobleman of Crossout.*

WiCkEd: *You removed my Night Assailant.*

ImginaryD00d: *End turn.*

I'll be honest with you, I use text dueling. (Text Dueling means using something like AOL Instant Messenger (AIM) to duel a buddy online). Does this mean I cheat? Heck no! I will be completely honest with you when we text duel, I would not cheat against you since it serves no overall help for myself.

What do I mean by this? Let me explain. If one cheats whilst dueling online they are not teaching themselves anything. By cheating online, they are changing the probability that they could draw "X" card.

A.) Why does this matter?

Say a Text Duelist Cheater went to a tournament a week after cheating online constantly. He plays, assuming he'd do well and loses every single match.

B.) Why?

The Cheater was being reliant on cheating when he dueled online and now ,in the real world, he's getting smacked around like a hobo in a bar fight.

C.) Why am I still rambling on?

It's important for you all to know that cheating online is bad. In fact, it is probably a sin in some Japanese Yu-Gi-Oh! handbook. When you cheat online, you learn nothing. You do NOT help yourself. And you obviously do not learn anything about your deck.

Online Duelist Rating: 10/10 (if you are playing with honest people)

Quality (with idiotic card abbreviations):6/10

Quality (without idiotic card abbreviations): 10/10

Overall: It's probably the MOST realistic and easiest form to obtain, given the fact you are not a cheater and don't play with cheaters.

Apprentice-Or the Multi-Talented and Multicomplicated

Apprentice is good. I won't exactly doubt it there. It was previously made for Magic: The Gathering players to test and play decks, and it has evolved into a few more card games including our loveable Yu-Gi-Oh! Apprentice has been around for a while. It's a pretty reliable way to play Yugioh Online with your friends. A few of the downside are as follows:

A.) Making Decks WILL Take You 20+ Minutes

This is probably the most irritating problem of all to me. I personally don't like spending that much time on a deck, some of you might, but I'm more of a guy who wants things fast and uncomplicated. If you don't mind the time constraints, it won't bother you, if you're impatient like myself, you'll be sort of irritated.

B.) Odd Symbols

I'm not sure if many of you have noticed, but there are some odd symbols you have to click on to move into other parts of Apprentice. This isn't so much of a bad thing as it is a confusing thing, entirely up to you.

C.) Lack of Players

Yeah, so this is one of the main problems, the lack of people that actually USE it. Granted you and a few friends might use it, but you aren't gonna find many other people who do. This REALLY takes down the viability of this program.

Online Duelist Rating: 6/10

Quality (with troubles):4/10

Quality (without troubles): 8/10

Overall: It's probably one of the more reliable, there really isn't much wrong with this outside those symbols and lack of players...plus the time you're going to spend in it.

Yu-Gi-Oh Online!: Erm...where ARE ALL THE DUELISTS?! yugioh-online.net

YGOnline seems to be a major flop to me. Here's a rundown. Yugioh Online is a Program you download from: www.yugioh-online.net. The Program is nice. It is "User-Friendly". But you have to pay to play. The Main Problems:

A.) Pay to Play

The pricing structure of "Yu-Gi-Oh! Online "is probably the strangest thing about the game. First off you have to pay to buy the program online. Then you have to pay again for every duel you participate in. This is very much a "turn-off" for most people.

B.) Obtaining Cards

A method of playing online should not also force you to play for several hundred hours to get the cards you want. We do enough rigorous card collecting in the real game.

C.) Lack of Players

Yugioh Online has almost no players, whilst, Magic The Gathering Online has thousands every day. Why did this happen to YGOnline? Well, Magic The Gathering has an older player base. Most of those people have credit cards, and don't mind paying to play a nice program. YuGiOh players are a younger crowd.

Online Duelist Rating: 6/10

Quality (with troubles):6/10

Quality (without troubles): 6/10

Overall: Nice Product, but expensive, and not many people to play.

So kids, there you have it. Keep in mind I AM NOT bashing your products, should you be the creator. Later!

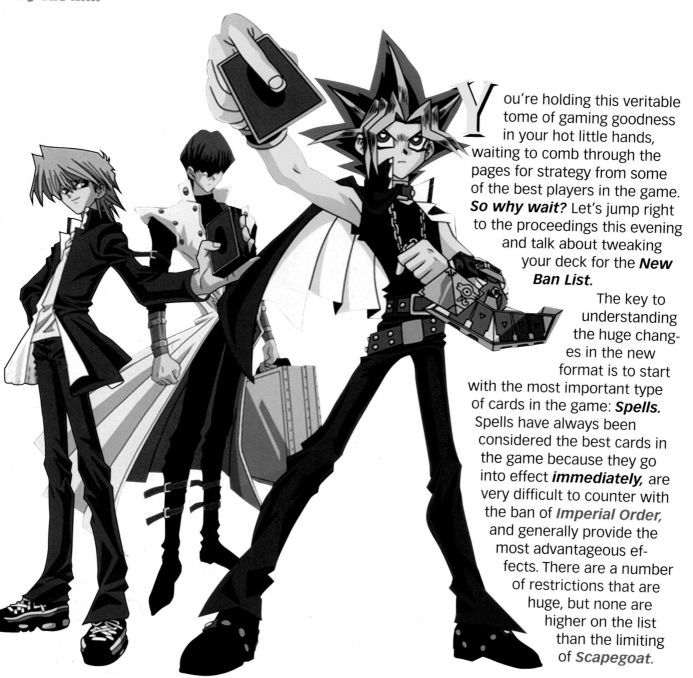

Tweaking Your Decks for the New Ban List

By: Jae Kim

Y ou're holding this veritable tome of gaming goodness in your hot little hands, waiting to comb through the pages for strategy from some of the best players in the game. *So why wait?* Let's jump right to the proceedings this evening and talk about tweaking your deck for the **New Ban List**.

The key to understanding the huge changes in the new format is to start with the most important type of cards in the game: **Spells.** Spells have always been considered the best cards in the game because they go into effect **immediately,** are very difficult to counter with the ban of *Imperial Order,* and generally provide the most advantageous effects. There are a number of restrictions that are huge, but none are higher on the list than the limiting of *Scapegoat.*

1S. The Loss of Scapegoat Makes Field Control Much Harder to Maintain

Prior to this shift, duelists could simply activate Scapegoat and bide their time, waiting to trigger monstrous advantage cards such as *Torrential Tribute* and *Lightning Vortex*. As a result of this, duels tended to stretch on past the twenty turn mark, mainly because life points were much easier to preserve. The restriction of Scapegoat obviously changes this mechanic; it has now become much harder to last a great amount of turns.

Most monsters that can break through the first wave of your opponent's defenses will now most likely punch through some damage. This makes beefy threats like *Injection Fairy Lily* or *Cyber Dragon* plus any normal monster even huger by comparison, since they'll likely be doing a third or more of your opponent's life points in one fell swoop. Other monsters with effects tied to battle damage like Don Zaloog, Spirit Reaper, and Masked Sorcerer have also become much, much better.

Duels will end quicker now, so you'd be wise to replace the loss of Scapegoat with as many playable traps and quickplay spells as possible to offset these losses.

2S. Scapegoat had Great Synergy with Metamorphosis and Book of Moon

Metamorphosis has now become a paradox. It was powerful enough to warrant restriction, but loses a lot of its power as a single copy because it has now become almost impossible to use it on a good effect. Before you could simply bring out multiple copies of Thousand-Eyes Restrict with relative ease; now having only one copy of each, along with probably one copy of Magician of Faith means that Metamorphosis will not get a great effect.

The 2000 attack monsters like *Ryu Senshi* and *Dark Balter the Terrible* have basically become obsolete with the release of Cyber Dragon. Your hard earned field presence will go poof; the only good targets appear to be Reaper on the Nightmare and Thousand-Eyes Restrict. However, expect to see such easy field control as Metamorphosis slowly start to fade from the landscape.

Book of Moon's loss is more subtle; Royal Decree centric builds are now more difficult to construct, but almost all decks lose equal utility with the loss of Book of Moon. Its versatility made the card fit seamlessly into almost any deck strategy; the restriction hurts everyone equally.

3S. Dark Hole and Heavy Storm are the new Delinquent Duo

The trinity is gone, replaced by the **two most advantageous cards left in the game.** *Heavy Storm* and *Dark Hole,* along with arguably *Snatch Steal,* are now the best cards in the game. Use them wisely, almost as fail safe resource evening buttons should you be down a few cards to your opponent. Proper conservation of Heavy Storm remains as important as ever, and Dark Hole should generate plenty of two for ones or more.

The other restrictions and returns are basically inconsequential. Deckout loses quite a bit with the restriction of Book of Taiyou, and Confiscation will not do that much to change the metagame. It's the most balanced out of the old three set of *"Pre-negators"* and thus should see play in every

side-deck, at least.

After the loss of key spells, the next thing everyone will notice is the simultaneous banning or restriction of some of the best monster cards to ever be printed, starting with the infamous Black Luster Soldier-Envoy of the Beginning.

1M. The Ban of BLS Helps Almost Every Non-Chaos Deck

The main **win condition,** able to do over 5000 damage in one turn, is now gone. This means that decks will have to generate a consistent stream of damage to end the game. Enter the second renewal of the beatdown era, where monsters will be steadily used to reduce life points **one battle at a time,** instead of in one fell swoop like the old format.

You **do not** need Light and Dark monsters any more; almost anything will do, so expect to see themes such as Gravekeepers, Zombies, and Warriors take precedence on the center stage. Inventive

users might try to run *Chaos Sorcerer,* which is still a great card in its own right, but Chaos as an entire tier one archetype is basically dead.

2M. The Ban of Sinister Serpent Hurts Every Deck and Fatally Wounds Others

The new school Water Control deck is dead, having lost its primary win condition. However, **almost every deck takes a painful beating with the loss of *Sinister Serpent,*** one of the best resource generators in the game. The ban of Serpent and BLS basically leaves only *Breaker the Magical Warrior* which completes the trinity of basically the best monsters in the game.

It is truly a shame because

the water deck had the makings of something really competitive. Unfortunately, it looks like water deck fans will have to go back to running A Legendary Ocean, which is not such a bad prospect. However, the loss of Sinister Serpent undercuts the value of Metamorphosis, Enemy Controller, Card Destruction…. You get the point. The restriction of Night Assailant does not entirely help matters.

It also makes the banning of Tribe-Infecting Virus entirely irrelevant.

3M. The Restriction of both Tsukuyomi and Magician of Faith is Overkill

Overkill is not necessarily a bad thing; in this case it might even be considered a great design choice. The restriction of one severely undercuts the other. The Saint Magician is already assaulted on all sides, having lost its favorite copies of Pot of Greed, Delinquent Duo, and Graceful Charity. Throw in

the fact that BLS is gone, and there's almost no reason to run a sole copy of Magician of Faith. Sure it's a great card, but it does not really make a difference.

And what good is a Tsukuyomi without being able to recur the effect of either Magician of Faith or Thousand-Eyes Restrict? Sure you can try to continually get a card like Magical Merchant or Mask of Darkness to go off, but the effect is not quite the same. Also, having only one copy of the card *drastically reduces* the chances of any Tsukuyomi lock type of combo to go off. This, in the long run, makes the card relatively insignificant except as a counter to the Monarchs, which is a huge plus still.

4M. Enter the Era of 2400 Attack Tribute Monsters.

You can say goodbye to great tributes like Airknight, Vampire Lord, and Ancient Gear Beast. Monarchs and Jinzo should reign supreme. The reason

for this, obviously, is *Cyber Dragon,* which absolutely runs over Vampire Lord and Airknight Parshath. It is clearly an unbalanced card, but one we must endure until the next restricted list.

In Closing

You can basically assume games will be quicker, with more of an emphasis on beatdown-flavored monsters and immediate one for one trades. There will be more topdecks, bluffing, and immediate resource swings due to a lucky Heavy Storm or Dark Hole draw.

And while the loss of Mirror Force and Ring of Destruction make most players cringe, they can easily be replaced by similar cards like *Sakuretsu Armor and Bottomless Trap Hole.* While Ring is indeed the best trap in the game, its replacements are fairly comparable.

It is now time for you to run out and build your own decks for the new format.

Happy dueling!

61

Traditional Format – Unleashed POWER!

By Ken Hartwick

Card Strategy

MAGICAL SCIENTIST

Many Advanced Format players would argue that Traditional Format depends more on luck and that Advanced Format involves more skill.

Suppose for a minute that you're going out tonight to see a movie. You want to be entertained by something packed with action and excitement. There are two movies for to choose from. One of them has speeding rocket cars and jets with plenty of explosions and a hero who has to navigate traps with spikes, pits of snakes and friendly looking creatures that morph into slimy fire breathing demons. The other movie is similar, but the rocket cars are slow and explosions have been limited to two. The second movie also banned any scenes that have snakes and demons. Which movie do you think will be more entertaining?

First and foremost we play Yu-Gi-Oh! because it's fun, entertaining and challenging. In Yu-Gi-Oh! there are now two different formats under which we play, Traditional Format and Advanced Format. Which one is more fun, entertaining and challenging? If you want to go see the movie that was made without any restraints, you might also want to think about playing **Traditional Format Yu-Gi-Oh!**; the format in which there are **no banned cards**.

A few years ago there was no such thing as Advanced Format or Traditional Format. Likewise, there were no banned cards. In the first ban, players lost the use of 13 cards. The original ban list was composed of: *Chaos Emperor Dragon – Envoy of the End, Sangan, Witch of the Black Forest, Yata – Garasu, Dark Hole, Delinquent Duo, Graceful Charity, Harpies Feather Duster, Monster Reborn, Raigeki, United We Stand, Imperial Order and Mirror Force.* The October 2005 ban list revision brought the list up to 23 cards and the list is expected to grow into the future. Are the banned cards outrageously powerful? **YOU BET THEY ARE!** And that's exactly why you might have **more fun** playing Traditional Format Yu-Gi-Oh.

There are plenty of folks who like the Advanced Format which is most often played in tournaments. Many Advanced Format players would argue that Traditional

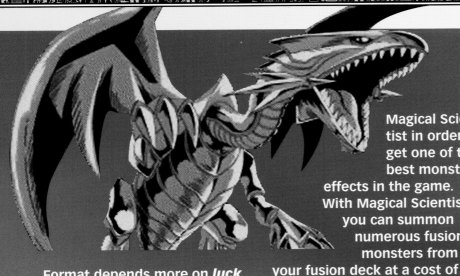

Format depends more on *luck* and that Advanced Format involves more *skill*. There might be more luck involved, but this is one of the key elements that make Traditional Format play more exciting. Traditional Format is a *faster* paced game and players are more prone to the unexpected. Likewise, in Traditional Format players can spring a big surprise on their opponent more often. You and your opponent will be whipped around like a speeding roller-coaster. In Traditional Format all the power of all the cards can be unleashed in your deck!

Traditional Format presents players with the opportunity to summon some of the strongest monsters in the entire game of Yu-Gi-Oh. This doesn't really make the game any easier, since your opponent will have a deck full of very powerful monsters too. Here are some ideas on what monsters you might want to play and why.

Magical Scientist

Although Magical Scientist is a level 1 monster with an ATK of only 300, you'll want to run a Magical Scientist in order to get one of the best monster effects in the game. With Magical Scientist you can summon numerous fusion monsters from your fusion deck at a cost of only 1000 LP's each. One way you can use Magical Scientist to win is to summon monsters that have an ATK of more than 2000 and then use *Catapult Turtle* to *"launch"* them to the graveyard. It is possible to win in one turn using this strategy. Other powerful strategies that use Magical Scientist involve using *Dark Flare Knight* to summon *Mirage Knight* to do massive LP damage.

Yata-Garasu

Yata -Garasu is another seemingly small monster with a game winning effect. The trick to winning with Yata-Garasu is to clear your opponent's monster zones and then resummon Yata-Garasu each turn for a direct attack of 200 LP's. The part of Yata-Garasu's effect that makes it a game winning card is that each time you do this your opponent skips their next draw phase, meaning they *can't* get new cards to help them stop the 200 LP's of damage that they take each turn. This often forms a *"lock"* in which your opponent is unable to stop you from peaking away their LP's each turn until you win.

Chaos Emperor Dragon -- Envoy of The End (CED-EotE)

CED-EotE is a very different kind of monster. *It's huge and explosive.* CED-EotE's effect clears the field and hands of both players while doing massive damage to your opponent. Not only that, but it's a very easy summon if you build your deck with light and dark attribute monsters and it has a huge ATK of 3000. You can frequently win immediately after you summon this monster.

Black Luster Soldier -- Envoy of the Beginning (BLS-EotB)

My *favorite* monster in the list is BLS-EotB. It's similar to CED-EotE because it's summoned by removing a dark and light attribute monster from your graveyard and it has an ATK of 3000. But its effect is totally different, you can use it to attack twice or remove a monster on your opponent's side of the field from play. Most folks like to use BLS-EotB to attack twice since slamming your opponent with an ATK of 3000 repeatedly is very likely to win you the game fast.

You'll also be able to play some very powerful spell and trap cards in the Traditional Format and I'll recommend a few of them here along with some reasons why you might want to add them to your Traditional Format dueling deck.

Change of Heart (CoH)

This card is just amazing and can often *win you the game.* You get to take your opponent's monster for free so they are minus one monster and you are plus one monster. After you attack your opponent with it, you can use it to perform a tribute summon so that when your opponent gets it back, it's in their graveyard! If your opponent has a Magical Scientist, CED-EotE or BLS-EotB you can use CoH to take their monster and exploit their very powerful effects for your benefit.

Raigeki

With a single play you can wipe out all of your opponent's monsters. Raigeki is amazingly powerful and can set you up for a full turn of inflicting direct damage on your opponent. It's also a very *simple* card to use, just play it before your battle phase and you'll be in a great position.

Pot of Greed (PoG)

Free cards. PoG is even easier to use than Raigeki. When you draw it, play it and draw two more cards.

64

Everyone who plays a Traditional Format deck should be running PoG in their deck.

Ring of Destruction (RoD)

This is a personal favorite. RoD destroys one of your opponent's monsters and gives you a way to wipe out some of their LP's **at the same time**. You might not like the fact that you lose LP's too, but it's a small price to pay for combined monster destruction and LP loss during your opponent's turn.

Mirror force

You'll frequently end your opponent's turn by activating Mirror Force. Destroying all your opponent's attack position monsters is priceless and can often bring you from a near loss to a win. If you set a Mirror Force make sure to remember that you can **only** activate it when your opponent declares an attack.

Imperial Order (IO)

You can activate this at the beginning of your opponent's turn following the turn you set it. Once you do this, they **cannot** play any spell cards during their entire turn. While you can never be completely certain of what spells your opponent is getting ready to play, IO can give you an extra turn to setup a game winning play.

Know Your Cards

Before you get all excited about the power you can unlock in your Traditional Format deck, you need to remember that your opponent just might be playing these powerful cards too. So here are some thoughts about the vulnerabilities of some of these cards. Knowing the vulnerabilities of your cards and your opponent's cards is a key bit of wisdom that separates beginners from experts.

Your One Two Punch

Two of the best cards in the entire game that can get rid of huge overpowering monsters are *Bottomless Trap Hole* **and** *Torrential Tribute*. You also should consider RoD. The great thing about these cards is that you can use them on your opponent's turn after they've summoned a powerful monster. Mirror Force is also good for turning the tide on your opponent. Your opponent will be stunned that rather than getting two attacks of 3000 each from their newly summoned BLS-EotB, you've destroyed it and all their other attack position monsters. Other cards that extremely powerful monsters are vulnerable to include; Exiled Force, D.D. Warrior Lady, Dark Hole, CoH and Injection Fairy Lily.

The best way to **stop** the overpowering spell cards that Traditional Format offers is with IO. You can activate it on your opponent's turn for free. The 700 LP cost doesn't start until your turn and you have the option to destroy IO rather than pay the LP's. You also might want to use Breaker the Magical Warrior and Heavy Storm against your opponent's spell cards.

The traps can be tough to deal with, but *Jinzo* **and** *Royal Decree* are pretty effective cards that you should think about running in your Traditional Format deck. I'd also recommend Harpies Feather Duster which is a must because it clears all your opponent's spell and trap cards in one swipe. You should also have a *Mystical Space Typhoon* in your deck.

Traditional Tricks

Traditional Format also offers ways to deal with powerful cards your opponent might be getting ready to play. You can play *Fiber Jar* to reset the game. This wipes out everything on the field and in both players hands. You can also wipe out the entire field by using the effect of CED-EotE. You also might want to play *The Forceful Sentry* which lets you look at your opponent's hand before you send one of their cards back to their deck. Delinquent Duo is also only playable in Traditional Format and it depletes your opponent's hand by two cards. Finally, you might consider running Confiscation which lets you look at your opponents hand before you select a card to send to their Graveyard.

Unleash the Fun

So have fun and don't let highbrow advanced players tell you what you can and cannot play. Being able to takeout your opponent's BLS-EotB is a very respectable feat and you only get to do that when you unleash the power of all the cards while playing Traditional Format Yu-Gi-Oh.

65

⏵⏵ Card Strategy ⏴⏴

The Newbie's Guide to Deckbuilding

New Players: Learn how to hold your own against the pros!

By: Michael Lucas

Every newbie's gone through it – a player just starting Yu-Gi-Oh (or any other card game), going to sit down for a game against a tournament regular, and within six turns, the fresh blood is out of cards and out of luck. It's a very discouraging sight for any player who's starting out and wants to take a serious interest in the game. But this is simply how things go at first. The player doesn't know the intricacies of the game, nor do they have the appropriate cards that can handle what the veterans are throwing at them. ***This doesn't have to be the case anymore, however.*** Better cards are available to players as commons, and almost every single card to make a tournament-worthy deck can be had for ***under $200;*** a deck coming very close to that could even go under $100. There are a few things every newbie should know when it comes to YGO, and I'll go over them by monsters, spells, traps, and other general ideas. If you haven't been playing in official tournaments

DON ZALOOG

[WARRIOR / EFFECT]
When this card inflicts Battle Damage to your opponent's Life Points, you can select and activate 1 of the following effects.
● select 1 card from your opponent's hand randomly and discard it to the Graveyard.
● Send 2 cards from the top of your opponent's Deck to the Graveyard.

ATK/1400 DEF/1500

or you just saw *Yu-Gi-Oh! GX* and want to get started in this game, hopefully this article will help you out on your path to becoming the new *"King of Games."*

Monsters

Ahh, the monsters, the core of Yu-Gi-Oh! itself.   There are so many choices available to us now. The game has changed *a lot* from when *Legend of Blue-Eyes* was the only set available, when basically the monster with the strongest attack score was going to win. Things are different now. *"Effect monsters"* rule the roost, and I can't remember the last time I've seen a super-strong deck using monsters without effects. But what makes a monster good or bad? Here are some *basic* ideas on what you might want to use:

● **Monsters that get rid of other monsters when they are destroyed**
For example. *D. D. Assailant* **and** *D. D. Warrior Lady* can get rid of stronger monsters as they remove themselves and whatever destroyed them from the game. For getting rid of face-downs, *Mystic Swordsman Lv. 2* is the absolute best; for getting rid of defenders, *Drillroid* can help out as well.

● **Monsters that destroy your opponent's cards or discard from their hand**
Don Zaloog can discard from the opponent's hand whenever he does damage; *Exiled Force* can sacrifice himself to get rid of any other monster. By reducing the number of cards your opponent has, you have a better chance of winning.

● **Cards that generate an advantage**
Two very well-known cards that give an advantage are *Sangan* **and** *Breaker the Magical Warrior*. Breaker can destroy an opposing

◄◄ Card Strategy ◄◄

BRAIN CONTROL

[SPELL CARD]

Pay 800 Life Points. Select 1 face-up monster on your opponent's side of the field. Take control of the selected card until the End Phase of the turn this card is activated.

Spell or Trap and still destroy a monster in the same turn, giving a 2 for 1 advantage; when Sangan goes from the field to the graveyard, you can add another monster with 1500 Attack points or less from your deck to your hand. When you use one card to do 2 things, that's generally a good card.

• Elemental searchers

Basically, any card that says *"When this card is destroyed as a result of battle, you may Special Summon 1 (insert type here) monster with an ATK of 1500 or less from your Deck in face-up Attack Position. The deck is then shuffled."* This can either protect you (as you can pull another copy of the same card that was destroyed) or help

accelerate a strategy (a Mystic Tomato can search out a Don Zaloog after it's destroyed, and the Don Zaloog can try to discard a card from the opponent's hand.) Almost any card that **replaces itself** after it's destroyed in battle is a solid choice.

However, there are a couple things to watch out for with monsters:

• Too many Tribute monsters

This is the **number one** mistake I see from new players. The more tribute monsters that are played in a deck, the higher chance there is that you'll be stuck with them in your

hand without any way to put them on the field. A general guideline is to **run 2 monsters with a tribute cost** unless you are running additional ways to help pay for that cost (like Brain Control, which could take an opponent's monster, which would allow you to tribute it to summon one of your own.)

• Monsters with high costs or that require a discard to activate an effect

Cards like *Cybernetic Magician* may seem good at first glance, but by using the effect repeatedly, the player can run out of cards and an opponent who was conserving their cards can swing in to potentially win the game.

68

Spells

The game would be *boring* without spell cards. Without them we'd just be summoning a monster every turn and attacking for a few hundred damage each turn, until one person got an unbeatable monster out and would proceed to win the game. There are a few things players should have their spell cards do no matter what the deck type is – especially for newbies, who are best off learning with a deck where they just summon, attack, and use basic cards that they can understand easily. Here are a few examples of spell types that will come in handy:

- **Spells that destroy opponent's monsters**

Dark Hole, Smashing Ground, and Fissure are all great cards to get rid of face-up monsters. Nobleman of Crossout is the best for getting rid of face-downs.

- **Spells that destroy opponent's Spell and Trap cards**

Heavy Storm can get rid of all the Spell and Trap cards on the field, and Mystical Space Typhoon can get rid one specific card. *Both should be in any new player's deck*.

- **Cards that protect a player from being attacked**

Book of Moon, Enemy Controller, and Scapegoat are all Quick-Play Spells, meaning that if you set them on the field, you can use them during the opponent's turn. Scapegoat can give you four monsters to endure opponent attacks; Enemy Controller and Book of Moon can both stop an attack by shifting the opposing monster to defense position (except Book of Moon also turns it face-down.) Swords of Revealing Light is also another classic card that can buy a player on the ropes a few turns to get the cards they need to come back.

69

◂◂ **Card Strategy** ◂◂

• Cards that benefit a deck theme

The **king** of theme deck support is, without a doubt, *Reinforcement of the Army.* Being able to search your deck for any Level 4 or lower Warrior monster can give you an answer to quite a few situations. Gravekeeper decks have Necrovalley, which not only boosts the Gravekeeper monsters but also prevents the use of cards in the Graveyard. Harpie decks have Harpies' Hunting Ground, which can destroy opposing Spell or Trap cards throughout the Duel.

And finally, *Premature Burial and Snatch Steal should be in almost every deck ever made;* bringing a destroyed monster back or taking an opponent's monster are very powerful effects.

There are two other Trap cards that should be in almost every deck: Call of the Haunted and Torrential Tribute.

Traps

Traps are like sweets; they can be very good but **too many** at once isn't. There are several ways to get rid of trap cards and other ways to stop them from working, so relying on traps alone isn't a great idea. For the new duelist, they should do a very small, specific set of things:

• Destroy an opponent's monster who is trying to attack

Many players are running 2 or even 3 copies of *Sakuretsu Armor,* which destroys an opponent's monster who is trying to attack. You give up your one trap card to get rid of their powerful monster – a great trade-off.

• Destroy or remove opponent's monsters when they're summoned

Bottomless Trap Hole is a great card that can not only get rid of an opponent's strong monster but remove it from the game.

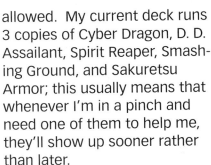

- ## Destroy your opponent's Spell or Trap cards before they get a chance to use them

One Mystical Space Typhoon and one Heavy Storm aren't enough to get rid of all of your opponent's Spell and Trap cards for an entire Duel. A couple copies of *Dust Tornado* should fill in the rest – a player can use them to clear out the opponent's spell or trap cards before they launch a flurry of attacks that would otherwise be stopped by Sakuretsu Armor or something.

There are two other Trap cards that should be in almost every deck; *Call of the Haunted and Torrential Tribute.* If Premature Burial is good, and it costs 800 Life Points to use, then Call of the Haunted is just as good, as it does the same thing but for free! The only catch is that you have to set it and wait a turn, just like with all Traps. (This is the number one mistake I see with trap cards – even players who have experience with other card games tend to try to play traps face-up from their hand.)

Conclusion

I'd like to give a few more pieces of advice to the beginning player, so that they won't have to go through the hardships that most other newbies do when starting this great game.

Check the Forbidden and Restricted lists to make sure your deck is legal! Some very commonly played cards, along with some cards we've grown up with seeing players use in the show, have been banned – Monster Reborn, Pot of Greed, and Mirror Force can no longer be used. The last thing you want to do is go to a tournament and be turned away as you were trying to use illegal cards.

Consistency is a good thing. If a card really helps you, and it's not restricted at all, it's usually a good idea to run 3 copies of it, the *maximum* that you're allowed. My current deck runs 3 copies of Cyber Dragon, D. D. Assailant, Spirit Reaper, Smashing Ground, and Sakuretsu Armor; this usually means that whenever I'm in a pinch and need one of them to help me, they'll show up sooner rather than later.

And finally, pick up a couple of the newer *Structure decks,* even if you already have an older Starter deck – ESPECIALLY the Warrior's Triumph. New players will have a much easier time getting cards that used to be reserved for the rich or lucky players – Royal Decree, D. D. Warrior Lady, Torrential Tribute, Call of the Haunted…almost all of the cards we use today that were $20 cards in the past can be picked up for dirt cheap.

Good luck Newbies!

71

Top 10 Burn Cards

By: Lord Tranorix

Burn may seem like a pretty straightforward term, but there are quite a few ways to define it. To avoid confusion, I'm making this list the top 10 cards – in the current Advanced Format – that actually cause damage to your opponent's Life Points.

1) Ceasefire

I've always loved Ceasefire. It stops Flip Effects and it can do up to 5000 damage (and though that's unlikely, 2500 isn't). It's also fun to use with cards like Tsukuyomi and Nightmare Penguin, who still get their effects. Best Burn ever!

2) Wave-Motion Cannon

Keep your opponent from destroying it and the game is yours in eight turns; fewer still, if it's later on. Even launching Wave-Motion Cannon to do a mere 2000 or 3000 damage isn't that difficult, and it can easily turn around the game.

3) Cannon Soldier

If Burn has an apotheosis of versatility, it's Cannon Soldier. Though he lost some power with Scapegoat's restriction, he can still launch a plethora of rentsy monsters, and he's still a great come-from-behind finisher.

4) Magic Cylinder

Say what you will, Magic Cylinder is still a rentsy card, especially in Burners. The ability to deal game-winning damage with one tiny little card is amazing. It isn't chainable and it doesn't give you card advantage, but sometimes Life Points matter more.

5) Stealth Bird

1700 DEF and a reusable effect that deals 1000 damage per turn? Yes please! Virtually a Burn Staple, Stealth Bird occasionally even finds its way into non-Burners. If your opponent can't deal with it quickly, Stealth Bird may well win you games.

6) Chain Energy

This isn't for every Burner, but if you put it in the right deck, your opponent will hate you forever. Using Chain Energy is all about strategy; make sure you plan your deck well, because trust me: 500 Life Points per card WILL ADD UP.

7) Solar Flare Dragon

1500 ATK isn't great, and 500 damage per End Phase isn't fantastic either; but the fact that having two of these on the field is tantamount to permanent stall – PLUS 1000 damage per turn – makes Solar Flare Dragon quite a rentsy monster.

8) Lava Golem

Great card, yes, but I don't think Lava Golem deserves to be higher. Sure, it's both monster removal and Burn, but if your lock falls apart, you'll be hurting. Lava Golem's also very easy to counter; a simple Book of Moon will do it.

9) Des Koala

What's there not to love about a monster with a respectable 1800 DEF who can do potentially massive damage? There are few joys greater than when an unsuspecting opponent attacks this with a huge hand; it's not uncommon to do 2000 damage.

10) Secret Barrel

Often overlooked, Secret Barrel can be a valuable addition to Burn Decks. If you go first and draw this, you're more than likely guaranteed 1200 damage; playing it after a Cyber Jar or something can make it do even more. Plus, it's chainable!

73

Top 10 Card Advantage Cards
The cards that will give you a leg up in the new format!

By: Michael Lucas

Top Ten Lists

As we all know, the new Advanced Format list is upon us. Cards that used to give us an instant advantage are gone, such as Delinquent Duo and Graceful Charity (and thanks to Upper Deck, we've lost Pot of Greed as well). In addition, Sinister Serpent, the infinite advantage card, is gone as well, so players will actually have to pay for their discards now. But there are still a few cards that are better than all others at making sure you have more cards than your opponent. Having said that, here are the Top 10 cards that generate advantage:

1 and 2 (tied): Heavy Storm and Dark Hole

These two are the king and queen of advantage; these two cards can clear the entire field on their own. An opponent who overextends by putting 3 Traps down and 3 monsters on the field can easily be humbled by these two little lifesavers. These two are tied as both are equally important and both should be seen in every deck in existence.

3: Torrential Tribute

With Mirror Force and Ring of Destruction gone, Torrential Tribute is the single best Trap card we have left and the only one that can potentially save you from a major onslaught. Destroying 2 or 3 monsters with this is game-breaking.

4: Snatch Steal

Not counting the life point cost, it's a +2 (your opponent loses 1 monster from their field and you gain 1 monster), with possible extra advantage if you either use the stolen monster's effect to your advantage or sacrifice it for a Tribute or an effect.

5: Breaker the Magical Warrior

Breaker is a more basic 2 for 1; he's a monster and a Mystical Space Typhoon packed into the same card. Although the monster that's left behind isn't necessarily strong, if he destroys an opponent's spell or trap, then destroys a monster, he served as a 2 for 1.

6: D. D. Assailant

This little Warrior should be, at worst, a 1 for 1 – either your opponent destroys it in battle (and loses their monster) or has to waste a removal card on it (Sakuretsu Armor, Smashing Ground.) Hopefully, DDA will destroy an opponent's monster or two before being taken out, generating extra advantage.

7: Sangan

Despite the lower number of cards that can be searched by this guy now, it's still an extra card in hand. This card also turns your Premature Burial and Call of the Haunted into 2 for 1's, as not only are you getting a monster but another search when Sangan is destroyed again.

8: Mobius the Frost Monarch

It's a 2 for 2 – the monster you tributed and the Mobius from your hand for 2 Spell/Trap cards on the field. But this is a very important 2 for 2, as monsters are easier to come by than Spell/Trap removal.

9: Magician of Faith

Although she's only a 1 for 1, it's a very weak card getting back a very strong one. The best card advantage cards we have left in the game are Spells, so getting back one of these for a second use can be devastating.

10: Confiscation

This isn't card advantage on its own, but if you know what your opponent has, especially in the first or second turn, you can plot your moves accordingly so that other cards you have can generate advantage.

75

Top Ten Lists ▸▸

▸▸ Top Ten Lists

Top 10 Cards To Revisit With the
New Ban List

By: Jae Love

T This Top 10 List is based on the new October 1, 2005 Banned & Restricted List. Here are 10 cards you may want to re-look at for your deck.

1. Mobius the Frost Monarch

This card is absolutely huge in the new format. With almost every trap being downgraded to unchainable, you can find your new 2400 attack best friend creating huge two for one swings that can often decide the game.

2. Cyber Jar

The emphasis on beatdown forces requires a few reset buttons. Sure you've got Dark Hole and Torrential Tribute, but why not throw in this nifty Dark monster for an extra kick?

3. Magical Hats

The loss of Scapegoat leaves open the door for all sorts of filthy combos involving Dark Coffin and Statue of the Wicked. Run multiple copies of Magical Hats to get instant two for one trades!

4. Injection Fairy Lily

Games are put on a limited turn timer with this bad girl in play. She can definitely cut short your opponent's defenses by smashing through for 3400 damage in a single battle phase.

5. Smashing Ground

The instant one for one trade form of monster removal will be seen in almost every deck. Monster removal is necessary more than ever in a heavy beatdown based format.

6. Goblin Elite Attack Force

This is the most reliable non-tribute monster counter to the heavily played Cyber Dragon. 1500 defense will enable it to stand up to some abuse after punching a hole through your opponent's strongest piece.

7. Don Zaloog

Easy access to direct attacks because of the restriction of Scapegoat helps Don Zaloog shine in decks that need more attack power. You'll choose between this and Spirit Reaper depending on how much damage you need.

8. Kinetic Soldier

A great way to counter the expected surge of Warrior decks. Kinetic Soldier used to see play in many a side deck before gradually disappearing; it is definitely back.

9. Creature Swap

The restriction of Scapegoat leaves open the door for this once powerful spell to return to the fray. Use it with elemental searchers like Mystic Tomato for maximum effect.

10. Mirror Wall

This is a great card in conjunction with damage based monster effects like Don Zaloog and Airknight Parshath. Experiment with it; you might like it more than Sakuretsu Armor!

77

Top 10 Commons

By: Ryoga

Everyone has piles of commons hidden away in a shoebox. They generally aren't useful, but a few stand out. Here is a selection of some of the best you can currently use in a deck. These are great commons and are proud of it!

1. Smashing Ground

A strong one-for-one trade, this is. Evil monsters generally have a high DEF, so you're generally going to destroy that which you like least, and when the only thing in your way is one monster, it won't be there for long.

2. Gravekeeper's Spy

The reason Gravekeepers work. 2000 DEF is a mighty wall, so your opponent will have to use something like Smashing Ground to destroy this, keeping your better monsters safe. He is a great swarm card, as you can reuse his ability with Tsukuyumi.

3. Sakuretsu Armor

Now that Mirror Force is gone, many will use two or three copies of this. Unlike most monster destroyers, you can choose your target. The only drawback is you have to wait for an attack. It is a must have for any deck not using Royal Decree.

4. Zombyra the Dark

An asset to weenie warrior decks and Deck Devastation Virus. He utilizes the strong Warrior support and has a huge ATK. It does decrease, but he should remain a threat long enough. Great for destroying Vampire Lords and Berserk Gorillas!

5. Armed Samurai – Ben Kei

A card so powerful he needs his own deck. He works like this: 1. Play Giant Trunade to clear the backfield; 2. Play Ben Kei; 3. Play three or four Equip Spell Cards. Four attacks with 3000+ ATK should finish any game.

6. Level Limit – Area B

A widely used stall card. Most decent monsters are Lv.4 or higher. You can then play a Lv.3 monster, like Jerry Beans Man, and attack anyway. It is likely to be destroyed, but you have cards like Magic Reflector to help deal with that.

7. Trap Dustshoot

Popular with advanced players, but anyone can use it. Just set it on the first turn and chain to your opponent's draw. We have few control cards left, and removing a monster helps stall the game. Also, it is not prone to being negated by Royal Decree.

8. Wave Motion Cannon

Used to bait Spell and Trap removal away from something useful. It also gives aggro decks some zest. Play this and your opponent stops trying to win, but starts trying to destroy this. A necessity for burn decks.

9. Swarm of Locusts

One the reusable Flip effect monsters. This can be fetched with Mystic Tomato or Howling Insect. Destroying Spells and Traps is very powerful, and the longer you keep this guy alive, the better he gets.

10. Thunder Dragon

The classic deck thinner, this helps other cards work. You put Light monsters in your Graveyard, have cards to discard for costs, and reduce your deck size. However, it is a horrible topdeck and drawing two is painful.

79

The Top 10 Fiends!

By: YamiBakuraFan

Top Ten Lists

Fiend monsters have been an ever present dark force in the Yu-Gi-Oh! Trading Card Game. Fiend decks are very popular with a variety of players and support many different game play styles. Here I will compose a list of the top ten fiend monsters and give a brief explanation as to why they are so good.

01) Sangan

Sangan is single-handedly the best searcher in the entire game in the current advanced format. Unlike other deck searching monsters, Sangan will get its effect straight from the field rather then being limited to being destroyed in battle.

02) Night Assailant

Even though this card works a lot better in sets of two or three, Night Assailant can be abused even when limited. It will work like a Man-Eater bug for some quick removal when set and can get back your vital flip monsters when discarded.

03) Newdoria

The main source of field removal in a fiend deck comes from Newdoria. It works a lot like a D.D. Assailant and can be specially summoned from your deck with Mystic Tomato. All fiend decks should use two or three.

04) Dark Jeroid

This is Newdoria's half brother works equally as well in certain situations. The loss of 800 attack can make a monster very vulnerable. Jeroid is also a good target for Mystic Tomato!

05) Dark Ruler Ha Des

Ha Des is a powerful fiend. With his 2450 attack points, he can trump almost every high level monster being used in decks nowadays. He also transforms all of your fiends into effect negators which can seriously hinder your opponents strategies.

06) Dark Necrofear

The card that single-handedly created the fiend deck. Since it's a special summon, it can be brought out quickly and has a great attack and defense as well. When destroyed, it becomes a free Snatch Steal and will give you control of an opponents monster!

07) Slate Warrior

An easily abused beat down card. If you flip it up you get a non-tribute 2400 attacker! This is rare but good nonetheless. Its other effect can help to weaken your opponents monsters.

08) Terrorking Archfiend

Although this card is very hard to summon, once it hits the field it will stick around for awhile. Terrorking is a mini Dark Ruler Ha Des and with its dice roll effect can avoid your opponents pesky magic and traps.

09) Goblin Elite Attack Force

A huge beatstick monster that laughs at cards like Cyber Dragon and Vampire Lord. Best of all when Goblin goes to defense its 1500 defense will protect it from being easily destroyed like its warrior counterpart.

10) Giant Germ

A great burn and swarm engine that is overlooked by many players. Germ can grant easy field advantage and helps get fiends into your graveyard for your Dark Necrofear, not to mention its good synergy with Creature Swap as well.

Top Ten Lists

81

Top 10 (Advanced Format) Dark Monsters

By: WiCKEd

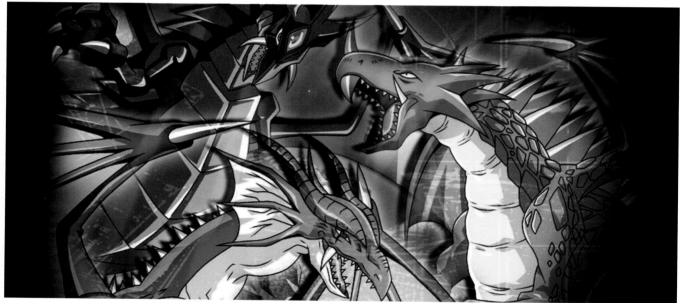

1. Breaker The Magical Warrior

He's still our best Dark Monster no matter what format. He comes out as a 1900/1000 stat monster. Also has the ability to remove the counter (which added 300 ATK) to destroy 1 Magic or Trap on the field. You could end up destroying an infamous Sakuretsu Armor, Scapegoat, or something else like a Royal Decree. So, you have what many know as the best "topdeck" (monster-wise) in the game as our number one rank.

2. Sangan

Our favorite searcher takes spot number two. Sangan's stats are not impressive at 1000/600, but he is a Fiend, so after you search he can be Necrofear fodder.

Sangan can search out nice cards like D.D. Warrior Lady, Spirit Reaper, Mystic Tomato, or a barrage of other monsters to your hand.

3. Spirit Reaper

Ah, the Reaper. Don't fear the Reaper. Use it! This is a staple in Tomato Control decks for the ability to have a solid, stable defense without worries of death and doom in the next turn. Downside of Reaper is his vulnerablity to Enemy Controller or any other "designation" by other cards. He still holds the number three spot due to his massive defensive and possible disruption benefits.

4. Newdoria

Third Dark monster, for a few reasons. If he is destroyed by battle he lets you choose another monster to go down with him. You could choose a Don Zaloog, D.D. Assailant, Berserk Gorilla, anything, even facedown monsters. Realistically, Newdoria will always provide an advantage (unless killed outside of battle).

5. Don Zaloog

Ranked number five is the leader of the Dark Scorpion Gang himself, Don Zaloog. Don himself is a very well rounded monster for his effects. Yes, effects, he has 2. The first being the most beneficial to you most of the time, it's simple randomly discarding a card from your opponent's hand.

6. Exarion Universe

Alright, so Mr.Exarion's release was quite a bit late. Although I must say, I'd still use him even in the new format with the restriction of Scapegoat at 1. Exarion's stats are 1800/1900, meaning he's either a beatstick or defender, but unsearchable given any circumstance. I would inspire still testing him in the new format, he's worth while.

7. D.D. Survivor

He's the pinnacle of "anti-metagame". And by that I mean he's anti-Assailant and Warrior Lady. This is always good..considering Assailant is usually run in 2s or 3s, which is ridiculously annoying. Side deck 1, and possibly main deck1. He's worthwhile.

8. Mystic Tomato

Easily one of the BEST Dark monster of our new format. It searches out various monsters that can totally change the way the field is controlled and impacted. You can fetch Newdoria, Dark Jeriod, Don Zaloog, Spirit Reaper, or another Tomato...all of which impact the game in immense ways.

9. Tsukuyomi

S(He) was one of the biggest annoyances in the old Advanced Format along with Thousand-Eyes Restrict and became one of the centerpieces of the plague known as Goat Control. It's still quite the good card, as you can still reset Magician of Faith and you can still reset opponent's monsters you wish to destroy easier such as Phoenix. A great Combo Card.

10. Vampire Lord

The king of vampires himself is ranked number 10. Why? He can't be thrown into any deck and expected to be amazing. Now that he's able to be abused in threes I see the possibility of people flocking to Zombie decks ... although I still say 3 V.Lord is too many.

▶ **Top Ten Lists** ▼▼

Top 10 Warrior Toolbox Cards

What you should be searching with Reinforcements of the Army (RoTa)

By: Michael Lucas

Just about everyone in competitive Yu-Gi-Oh! has seen Warrior decks get even more powerful with the new format. They gain consistency from Reinforcement of the Army, which lets them search for any Level 4 or lower Warrior monster in their Deck. This lets them get the right card to handle the situation, making RotA the "toolbox" and each monster a "tool" that can come out of it. Here's a list of cards you consider for your Warrior deck if you're running 2 RotAs:

1. D. D. Assailant

It's the best of the best, and you can use 3 of it. A strong 1700 ATK, and if it gets killed it's taking something down with it. It's the perfect picture of consistency for a Warrior deck; between 3 of this and 2 RotA*, you'll almost always have one when you need it most.

*Pojo Thesaurus: RotA = Reinforcement of the Army

2. D. D. Warrior Lady

It's restricted to 1, so it's worth using RotA to search this out. Optional removal lets it do what DDA can't and get rid of opposing Sangans or Reapers. If she wasn't limited then she'd easily be #1.

84

3. Don Zaloog

The best search against an open field, a free shot with Don means a free hand discard. Don is usually a bad card to topdeck, but RotA lets him hide out in the deck until he's needed unless you happen to draw him first.

4. D. D. Survivor

D. D. Assailant and Warrior Lady are run in mass right now. This card not only gets around their effects but also circumvents Bottomless Trap Hole. It's an anti-metagame card you should at least consider running 1 of.

5. Exiled Force

"1 for 1's" are good in this format; using your X to take out a stronger monster or a face-down that could potentially hurt you is a great thing. It won't help you come back from behind, but it will help press an advantage.

6. Blade Knight

In a format where people are topdecking early, this guy's great. A player that draws this with nothing else in their hand or on the field suddenly has a 2,000 ATK flip-effect negator.

7. Goblin Elite Attack Force

Trample use is down, so his 0 Defense isn't as much of a problem. This card's great against Cyber Dragon, whose 2100 ATK and free special summon has been the bane of a few players in the new Advanced Format. 2300 beats out quite a bit except for the Jinzos and Mobiuses (Mobii?) that are running around.

8. Mystic Swordsman Lv. 2

For those who need even more face-down removal. A single copy usually finds its way into the standard Toolbox; multiples may be in the side deck to counter the burn/stall decks that abuse face-down monsters.

9. Zombyra the Dark

He's a great opening play, standing up to almost all non-tribute monsters and can take out a Cyber Dragon where needed. Although not being able to directly attack hurts, it's better to send him against opposing beatsticks than something that could otherwise get in a clean shot at the opponent's life points.

10. Command Knight

A Warrior-booster who can also mess with the opponent's intended attack order is a good inclusion to a Toolbox. He's great against other Warrior decks that don't run him, as then your Don Zaloog will be able to take out their Don Zaloog for 400 points and a card in hand. He makes every other card further down the list that much more powerful.

▶▶ Top Ten Lists ◀◀

Top 10 Forbidden Cards
A list of the best of the banned!

By: Michael Lucas

The new Advanced Format is upon us, but it seems like only yesterday we were using our Trinities, discarding without really discarding, and removing a Light and a Dark from the Graveyard was usually the second to last thing to happen before a Duel ended. Although I do agree that this list is better than what were using from April 1 through September 30 of this year, I can't say I love all the card choices. Thus, I'll pay homage to the Top 10 cards you can't use anymore:

1: Yata-Garasu

This card is why the ban list was created. Before the first ban list, you either ran Yata or you lost, pretty much. You cleared their field, disrupted their hand, and the little bird finished 'em off.

2: Pot of Greed

It's the biggest advantage card we had. A free 2 for 1, no matter what. Although it is admittedly broken, I felt it was almost necessary, one card to let a player down to his last hope have a shot at coming back and winning.

Pojo Footnote:

* For those who complain about the unbanning of Dark Hole and Confiscation, just think what would happen if you had to deal with all of these. A final piece of advice about banned cards: you shouldn't get rid of every copy of them you own; you never know when the powers that be will allow them in competitive play again!

3: Black Luster Soldier - Envoy of the Beginning

Even though he doesn't destroy every card on the field, he usually ended up doing even more damage with two attacks (one of them direct). He's even more powerful then his draconic brother.

4: Chaos Emperor Dragon – Envoy of the End

A player who had no cards could draw this and win a game against a player who had ten. If the burn damage wasn't enough to win, comboing it with a Sangan and the #1 card on this list ensured it.

5: Harpie's Feather Duster

Spell/trap removal is even more difficult to come by, and this is the king of spell/trap removal. The costless destruction had to go.

6: Raigeki

Destroying every opponent's monster was just too powerful without a drawback. We have more balanced mass removal now, in Dark Hole and Lightning Vortex.

7: Delinquent Duo

Just like Pot of Greed, instead of where you give up one card to get 2, you get rid of 2 of your opponent's. When reused twice in the same duel, it was pretty much game over.

8: Magical Scientist

Although there are more powerful cards to look out for now, this was the basis of the most consistent First Turn Kill deck ever created; tweaked builds of that deck could win in one turn 90% of the time or more.

9: Fiber Jar

This card could pull a player out of the worst situations… and since it went back into the deck, it was there for another use, and another, and another. The constant reuse warranted its ban.

10: Imperial Order

This card was a far-too-easy way to shut down half of the opponent's deck, as people were playing 19-20 spells when it was legal. It would be even worse now without 3 Mystical Space Typhoons, except for those who play Royal Decree.

Top Ten Lists

87

Top Ten EEN Cards

By: Evan Vargas a.k.a. "SandTrap"

Top Ten Lists

With the release of the Elemental Energy set into the U.S. metagame, big changes have taken place. Dark World has become a new archetype, while other themes such as Elemental Heroes get a boost. With each new set, there are certain cards more powerful than others, and thus we have the Top Ten Elemental Energy cards!

Pojo Note:

Sandy cranked this article out about 1 month before EEN was released. EEN and this book will hit streets about the same time. Evan's Guideline will give you a "head start" on knowing which cards will impact the game. Translations are fan translations. Actual text and card images could vary from what actually hit U.S. soil.

1. Transaction of Darkness

EEN-052

Trap – Normal

Japanese Translation: This card can only be activated by paying 1000 life points when your opponent activates a Normal Spell card. The effect of that Spell card becomes "Discard 1 card randomly from your opponent's hand".

Transaction of Darkness is simply broken in a Dark World deck. For a mere 1000 Life Points, you can turn powerful Spells such as Heavy Storm and Dark Hole into blind Confiscations that could hit one of your powerful, effect-ridden Dark World monsters. And once it does, their special effects will activate, especially the effects of Gold and Silver!

2. Army God of Dark World - Silver

EEN-023

Dark/Fiend/5/2300/1400

Japanese Translation: When this card is discard into the Graveyard from hand by the effect of another card, special summon this card to your field. If this card is discarded by the effect of opponent's card, your opponent also chooses 2 cards in his/her hand and put them onto the bottom of his/her deck in any order.

Yet another powerhouse for the Dark World team, Silver's 2300 ATK can take down Cyber Dragon and anything else weaker than it. The effect is also incredibly powerful, and can be easily activated by the Number One card in Elemental Energy...

3. Military God of Dark World - Gold

EEN-024

Dark/Fiend/5/2300/1400

Japanese Translation: When this card is discard into the Graveyard from hand by the effect of another card, special summon this card to your field. If this card is discarded by the effect of opponent's card, also choose up to 2 cards on opponent's field and destroy them.

One of the powerhouse Dark World monsters, Gold packs a strong effect only matched by its ATK value. Players attacking with Spirit Reaper and Don Zaloog better pray not to hit this monster. Or use it in a combo with a powerful Trap card...

4. Barrier Passage Continuing to World

EEN-048

Spell - Quickplay

Japanese Translation: During the turn this card is activate, you cannot Summon, Reverse Summon, or Special Summon. Choose a monster with [Dark Realm] in your Graveyard and special summon it.

Monster Reborn for the Dark World decks, and as a Quick-Play Spell card! You can set this card and chain to your opponent's spell or trap removal during their turn to bring out a powerful Dark World monster while by-passing the negative part of the effect. Nice.

Top Ten Lists

89

Top Ten Lists

5. Scout of Dark World - Scar

EEN-025
Dark/Fiend/2/500/500

Japanese Translation: *When this card is destroyed as a result of battle and sent to Graveyard, choose a monster with [Dark World] in its name with level 4 or less from your deck and add it into your hand.*

Scar provides great versatility in a Dark World deck. Although the stats are weak, you can search for a Dark World monster to add to your hand, making sure that you'll have plenty of monsters to summon next turn.

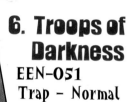

6. Troops of Darkness

EEN-051
Trap – Normal

Japanese Translation: *Choose 2 monsters with [Dark World] in your Graveyard and add it onto your hand.*

With the entrance of the Dark World monsters came plenty of supportive Dark World Spell and Trap cards. Troops of Darkness will give you card advantage while returning Dark World monsters back to your hand, where they are the most deadly.

7. Jar of Avarice

EEN-037
Spell – Normal

Japanese Translation: *Choose 5 monsters in your Graveyard and shuffle them into your deck. Afterward, draw 2 cards from your deck.*

Speaking of Banned cards, Pot of Greed was recently put down for good. A possible replacement could be Jar of Avarice. Early game, you may not be able to play this Jar right away, but mid to late-game it could be very powerful. Put back cards like Sangan and Breaker the Magical Warrior so you can use them again.

8. Hell Blast

EEN-050
Trap - Normal

Japanese Translation: This card can only be activated when a face-up monster on your field is destroyed and sent to Graveyard. Destroy the face-up monster with lowest attack strength on the field and each player receives damage equal to half of the attack strength of the monster destroyed by this card's effect.

Since Ring of Destruction is no more in the Advanced Format, some duelists may try using Hell Blast instead. After your opponent destroys one of your monsters, you can do the same right back, plus some Life Point damage that both players will remember. Be careful though, Hell Blast could backfire and destroy your own monster!

9. Nano Breaker

EEN-018
Earth/Machine/4/1600/1800

Japanese Translation: When this card attacks face-up monster with level 3 or lower, destroy it without doing Damage Calculation.

Annoying Spirit Reapers blocking your path? Scout of Dark Realm making you worried? Injection Fairy Lily too strong to take down? Now you worry no more, for with Nano Breaker, you can destroy these monsters easily. Solid ATK/DEF values make Nano Breaker a solid monster.

10. Level Limit Area A

EEN-060
Trap - Continuous

Japanese Translation: All monsters with level of 3 or less are switched to attack mode.

With Level Limit – Area A, Clown Control decks get a very welcome boost. Activate LL-AA and switch your Dream Clown into Defense mode. You'll activate its effect of destroying a monster on the field, and then go back into Attack mode, ready to destroy another monster next turn! Punish those Spirit Reapers as well.

Yu-Gi-Oh GX
Character Bios

By: Baz Griffiths

Yu-Gi-Oh! GX may have only just begun in America, but in Japan the second year has already started. Set some years after the end of Yu-Gi-Oh! the new series follows the students of the Duel Academy as they deal with classes, each other and the problems that come their way.

Meet the cast

Jaden Yuki

Jaden is a confident duelist with a strong fighting spirit, but was put into Slifer Red after humiliating Dr Crowler. Despite this, Jaden is determined to become the best duelist in his year, if not in the whole school. His close bond with his friends helps him through the hard times; however his tendency to break rules sometimes gets them in trouble too.

Alexis Rhodes

Alexis is one of the most talented female duelists in the Obelisk Blue dorm and shares a friendship with Jaden. She is an independent thinker but prefers to do things by the rules. Since her own brother disappeared from the academy, Alexis has developed a strong sisterly bond with Zane. However she has not given up finding him and is always looking for clues to help track him down.

Syrus Truesdale

Syrus and Jaden formed a strong friendship when the pair met during the entrance exams, and he thinks of Jaden as his big brother. Syrus has the potential to be a strong duelist but lacks the confidence in his own abilities. Hopefully sharing a room with Jaden will allow him to gain the skills he needs to progress as a duelist.

Animé Yu-Gi-Oh GX

Chumley Huffington

Chumley failed his first year exams last year and has been forced to resit the year. He is an optimistic person and his Australian themed deck has potential, however he never seems to be able to win when it really matters. But with his newfound friends he hopes to improve this year and pass that final exam.

Bastion Misawa

Bastion was one of the strongest duelists in this year's entrance exam and was placed into the Ra Yellow dorm as a result. Never one to be at a disadvantage in a duel, Bastion has constructed six decks to meet every eventuality. While he is much stronger than most of his fellow students, the only person he cares about beating is Jaden.

Chazz Princeton

The youngest of three brothers, Chazz is a student who believes that only the best should be admitted into the academy. He has rarely ever faced defeat and cannot understand how a low level duelist like Jaden could ever defeat him. But Chazz will have to pick up the pace or get used to the taste of defeat.

Zane Truesdale

Zane is Syrus's brother and top of the third year class. His strong performance means that few are able to rival him, let alone defeat him, and many say he has achieved perfection. But that doesn't mean Jaden won't try his hardest to end his reign and become the new number one.

Animé Yu-Gi-Oh GX

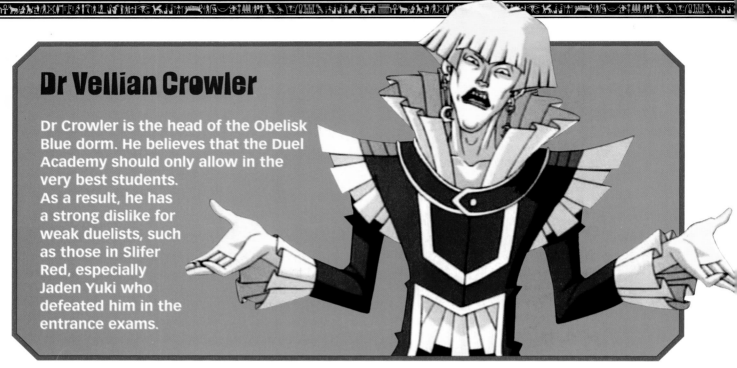

Dr Vellian Crowler

Dr Crowler is the head of the Obelisk Blue dorm. He believes that the Duel Academy should only allow in the very best students. As a result, he has a strong dislike for weak duelists, such as those in Slifer Red, especially Jaden Yuki who defeated him in the entrance exams.

Lyman Banner

Lyman is one of the teachers attached to the Slifer Red dorm. He seems to have a particular interest in Jaden, but his motives may not be entirely innocent.

Let the Classes Begin!

This is a summary of the important parts of the first year of Yu-Gi-Oh! GX. It does not include information on episodes that do not affect the overall storyline.

Please note: Some of the names used in these summaries are the Japanese names and will likely change when the show airs in the US.

As each new year begins, Seto Kaiba's Duel Academy holds entrance exams to find the best duelists from around the land. Running late for his exam, Jaden Yuki accidentally bumps into Yugi Moto on his way to the Academy. As the two duelists pick themselves up, Yugi offers the young duelist a card that he hopes will bring him luck – Winged Kuriboh.

Despite arriving late for the exams, Jaden is permitted to duel anyway and defeats Dr Crowler, the head of Obelisk Blue. In the process he meets two other candidates – Syrus Truesdale and Bastion Misawa. Bastion's strong performance in the exam means he is put in the Ra Yellow dorm, but Syrus's weak performance and Jaden's humiliation of Dr Crowler mean they are put into the Slifer Red with the drop out students.

Getting used to their new home Jaden and Syrus meet their roommate Chumley Huffington and the three quickly become friends. Determined to prove himself as a duelist, Jaden declares that he will do whatever it takes to become the best in the year. However his determination and skill cause problems with Obelisk Blue student Chazz Princeton and the pair quickly become rivals.

When Jaden and the others hear rumors of a haunted dorm they decide to investigate, finding themselves joined by Alexis Rhodes. Alexis explains that her brother was one of the people who once went missing from the dorm and she wants to know what happened to him. Investigating the building, Jaden is challenged by the mysterious Titan to a shadow duel. Discovering that Titan's powers are all an illusion Jaden is able to defeat him, but what he doesn't realize is that Titan was hired by Crowler in an attempt to get rid of Jaden.

Due to poor grades and losing against Jaden, Chazz is told that he must defeat Bastion to stay in Obelisk

Blue. Worried that he may let down his family's ambition of becoming the best duelist in the world, Chazz suggests that the loser of the duel must instead leave the academy. Using a water deck against Chazz's fire one, Bastion wins the duel easily but refuses to move to Obelisk Blue until he can defeat Jaden. Forced to keep his part of the agreement, Chazz leaves the academy without saying goodbye to the others.

Duel Academy Vs North School

As the annual duel between the Duel Academy and the North School approaches, Jaden and Bastion must duel each other to decide who will represent the academy in Chazz's place. Determined to defeat

Jaden, Bastion prepares his new, seventh deck especially for the duel. However when the pair face each other on the dueling field Jaden proves that he is the stronger duelist.

While the duel between Bastion and Jaden takes place, a mysterious journalist breaks into the island and discovers that Alexis' brother was part of a research project and that all the members disappeared. Although eager to release the information, he is dissuaded by Jaden's fighting spirit and decides to return to his true passion – dueling.

Elsewhere, Chazz finds himself washed ashore on an island where he meets a mysterious old man. With Chazz's deck ruined the man offers him a card, Ojama Yellow, to begin his new deck. He takes Chazz to the North School where he will be able to train but warns that he will need a full deck to enter. Searching the island Chazz is able to find a full deck of cards and enters the academy. Inside he is forced to duel every student in order to prove how strong he is. With his new deck Chazz is able to defeat every single student and is declared the academy's duel king and their new representative for the duel against the Duel Academy.

When the North School arrives for the duel, Jaden and the others are stunned to discover that their representative is Chazz. Chazz himself is shocked when his two brothers arrive, declaring that they are going to broadcast their little brother's victory to all of Japan. Although much stronger than before, Chazz is still unable to defeat Jaden and feels humiliated in front of his brothers, despite Jaden's insistence that winning isn't everything. Realizing that he still has a lot to learn Chazz decides to remain at the Duel Academy but is shocked when he hears he will have to

drop down to Slifer Red because he has missed three months of lessons.

The Seven Stars

Lyman Banner decides to take his Slifer Red class on a field trip to nearby ruins, and Alexis tags along hoping that the ruins may hold some answers to her brother's disappearance. The group ends up trapped in a shadow world where Jaden wins a mysterious pendant from the gravekeeper, securing the safe return of his friends in the process.

Called to the principal's office, Jaden, Alexis, Bas-

tion, Zane and Chazz are told that three Legendary Demon cards are sealed on the island, protected by seven keys. He gives the keys to Lyman, Crowler and the gathered students and warns them that seven powerful duelists – the seven stars – are approaching the island. The only way for the stars to take the keys is to win them in a duel, so each duelist must do their best to protect their key.

Darkness, the first of the stars, challenges Jaden to a shadow duel, in which the loser's soul will be sealed in a card. Jaden is able to defeat his opponent but the stress of the shadow duel leaves him weakened and in hospital. Darkness also collapses at the end of the duel, and Alexis is shocked to learn that he is her missing brother, Fubiki. The second star, Camilla,

Animé Yu-Gi-Oh GX

arrives to claim the keys and easily overpowers Dr Crowler in a duel. Furious that he was not allowed to duel Camilla first, Zane faces her and although the duel is close, Camilla's vampire deck once again proves too powerful.

With two keys lost to Camilla, Fubiki warns Alexis that she is the worst of the seven stars and that only somebody with a shadow item can defeat her. Using the pendant he received from the gravekeeper, Jaden is able to counter Camilla's own shadow power and finally defeats the second star.

When Chazz's brothers declare that they are buying the Duel Academy, he is forced to duel them using monsters with less than 500 attack points. Visiting a well which is full of weak cards Chazz finds two new Ojama cards – Ojama Black and Ojama Green. Combined with his own Ojama Yellow the three brothers prove a powerful combination and Chazz is able to defeat his brother

and prevent the purchase of the academy.

Bastion is challenged to duel Taniya, the third star, and although he stars well he is distracted by her claims that she loves him and loses the duel. Unable to cope with the defeat, Bastion loses his fighting spirit and Jaden is determined to get it back. Facing Taniya in a rematch Jaden shows what true spirit is and narrowly defeats the third star. After the remaining keys are stolen by a group of robbers, Chazz must duel the group's leader and the fourth star, Don Zaloog, in order to claim them back. Jaden is then confronted by the fifth star, the pharaoh Abidos the Third, and once again protects his key.

Still upset that her brother doesn't remember her, Alexis is shocked when Titan kidnaps her and takes her to the dorm where he lost to Jaden. Titan reveals that he now has real shadow powers and Alexis is quickly overpowered. Watching the duel Fubiki begins to remember his sister and his support helps her to overcome the sixth star. Pleased that her brother is back to normal, Alexis is shocked when Fubiki tells her that he was sent to the dorm by Lyman Banner and then kidnapped into the shadow world.

The Final Star

As Jaden and the others try to make sense of Fubiki's revelations,

Lyman mysteriously vanishes, adding strength to the belief that he is the last star. Separating to look for Lyman, Alexis and Chazz are both defeated by Amnael, the seventh star, who then challenges Jaden for the last key. As their duel progresses Amnael reveals that he became ill many years ago and used a fake body - Lyman - to stay alive. Amnael tells Jaden that even if he loses everything else he will still have friendship, but Jaden is determined not to lose and eventually defeats the final star.

With all the stars defeated, things begin to return to normal until Chazz tells Fubiki that he has feelings for Alexis. Deciding to help his friend in his quest for love, Fubiki and Chazz steal the seven keys and use them to challenge Alexis to a duel. Although angry that Chazz thinks he can win her love in a duel, Alexis accepts his challenge and defeats him.

Eruption

As the duel ends the volcano on the island begins to erupt and the gate starts to open. Realizing that Chazz has opened the gate by losing to Alexis, the group rushes to the gate to see the keys rise up from the ground. Before they can do anything the group is confronted by the academy's former chairman, Kagemaru. He explains that the cards could only be awoken by those with a strong spirit and that is why he set up the conflict be-tween the academy and the seven stars.

Taking the cards from the pedestal, Kagemaru challenges Jaden to one last duel which will fully awaken the demons. Realizing that Lyman sensed this would happen, Jaden puts his Philosopher's Stone card into his deck. Although the duel is tough, Jaden's faith in the strength of his deck pulls through and Kagemaru is defeated, once again sealing the Legendary Demons away.

After everything else that has come their way, Jaden and the others still have one final challenge to face – final exams. Chumley is told that he has won an Industrial Illusions contest and can become a card designer, but only if he proves himself in the practical exam. Facing Crowler in the final duel, Chumley puts all his faith in his Australia-based deck and manages the best performance of his life. Although he is eventually defeated by Crowler the professor allows him to take the position anyway, commenting that he has made great progress over the last year.

Exhibition Duel

With graduation approaching, the third year grades reveal that Zane is top of the class with full marks. Asked to choose his opponent for the exhibition duel at the end of the year, Zane asks that Jaden duel him in his final duel at the academy. The duel between the pair is close, eventually ending in a tie. Zane thanks Jaden for such a strong performance and tells him that he has no concerns about the future of the academy. But who knows what new challenges next year's students will bring with them when classes start all over again…

Yu-Gi-Oh: Nightmare Troubadour Review

By: Joseph "Otaku" Lee

Yu-Gi-Oh: Nightmare Troubadour is the first Trading Card Game simulation for the Nintendo DS. Let's see if this game lives up to the hype, or falls short.

Controls 4.0/5

Using the stylus and touch screen in conjunction with the d-pad and buttons seems to work best, though you can use just one or the other for the most part. Definitely a step up from previous games, even without the stylus. There are a few areas that can still use some polish, like "Yes/No" menus popping up in the middle of the screen, where it's easy to hit a card as well as your response.

Gameplay-3.75/5

If you aren't into TCGs, this game still might be fun. However, dueling semi-random opponents as you "wander" around the map gets a bit tedious. This is the most accurate I've seen the TCG represented, though there are still plenty of errors.

Graphics-3.5/5

Like the controls, we see probably the best ever for a portable Yu-Gi-Oh game. A mix of hand drawn and computer models, things look nice… except they don't move enough. Most Monsters have only a few frames of animation, and combat is just shaking and a slash mark. The story is told through still shots with text at the bot-

My room

Miracle of Nature

This pack contains many Insect-Type monsters, along with useful Flip Effect Monsters and Equip Spells. This pack is for beginner duelists.

80% collect

1 Pack/150 KCP

KCP 002630

Mystical Elf

[Spellcaster] A delicate elf that lacks offense, but has a terrific defense backed by mystical power.

光 LIGHT   ATK/ 800 DEF/ 2000

Magician Deck   ATK

tom of the screen. During duels, the split screen does help show the action better.

👁 👁 👁 👁

Sound-3/5

Just a little more than the basics: we have traditional "Yu-Gi-Oh" themed music, like you'd hear in the show (no lyrics) and generic "battle noises". Sufficient, but not as good as it could be.

👁 👁 👁

Story-3/5

A decent retelling of the "Battle City" and "Noa" story lines, with the obvious differences of much less detail and you as the main star. Instead of the actual finish for the Battle City Tour-

nament (the Alcatraz story Arc), Noa shows up sooner and you just head back to the mainland to eventually battle Yami Marik. We also get some extra characters from Duelist Kingdom added in too.

👁 👁 👁

Miscellaneous-3/5

There are some good extras: puzzles, mini-games, and extra modes. Unfortunately, all this is marred by a glitch in the game (that also appears to be in the Japanese version). Pegasus will disappear from the game if you don't unlock him as a regular opponent at just the right time.

Without him, you can't get all the deck lists or all the cards.

👁 👁 👁

Final Score-3.5/5

Yu-Gi-Oh: Nightmare Troubadour is a very solid game in general, and the best portable Yu-Gi-Oh game I have played. If it wasn't for the Pegasus glitch (and how it's been handled), this would probably be a must have for the Nintendo DS.

👁 👁 👁 👁

Yu-Gi-Oh: Nightmare Troubadour Walkthrough

By: Joseph "Otaku" Lee

Video Game Reviews ◀◀

Yu-Gi-Oh: Nightmare Troubadour is a fairly straightforward game that follows some show events, though loosely, and with you often replacing Yugi. The game includes an **excellent** reference section on how to play (in the game, head to the card shop), so below is some information to smooth out some of the rough spots for you, a few "*cheats*", and a warning about the infamous "*Pegasus Glitch*" that can keep you from completing (but not beating) the game.

the cards you'll begin with… but none of the cards determined this way are especially great. When Ishizu questions you later in the game, answering "*Power*" means a victory nets you Obelisk the Tormentor, while Slifer the Sky Dragon is yours if you answered "*Unity*". Also, if you duel Yami Yugi, he will occasionally offer to trade his Egyptian god card for

Tips, Tricks, and Warnings!

Decisions, decisions…

The game will ask you questions about your "*personality*" in the beginning of the game and later on when Ishizu is about to let you duel Kaiba for an Egyptian god card. When the game is starting, it's determining a few of

Japanese screens shown here.

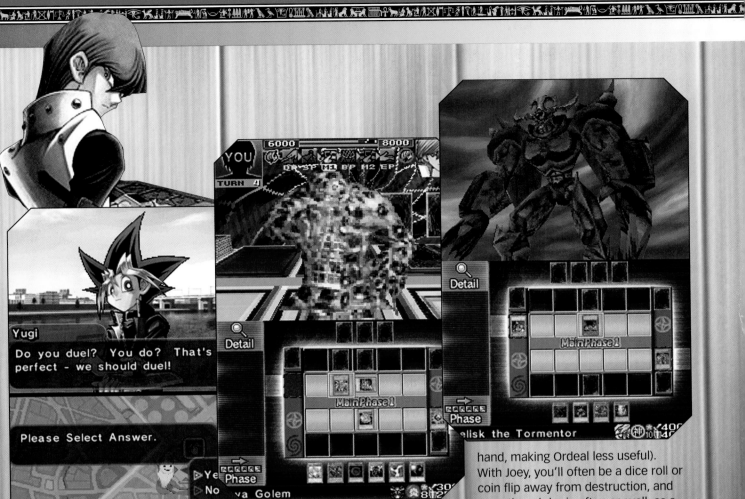

Yugi

Do you duel? You do? That's perfect - we should duel!

Please Select Answer.

▷ Ye
▷ No

yours. After you beat the game, keep dueling normal Marik for a chance at Ra (normal trading rules apply).

Starting At The Bottom...

Simply put, the starting deck you get regardless of your answers will still be very, very weak. Fortunately, so will the decks of most of your competition. However, there are some duelists that are definitely easier to handle then others. The game rates *Mokuba* **and** *Serenity* as Feeble, and it isn't kidding. It takes *a lot* of bad plays or misfortune in order to lose to them, but it *isn't* impossible so don't

let your guard down. Tea is just a hair stronger than them; mainly because she will occasionally get *Fire Princess* or a decent sized Monster out with good support. Still, these three are definitely the best opponents for you to focus on. Yugi Mutou and Bakura are pretty competent with solid decks, but as a whole they aren't *that* much better than you. The real threat early in the game comes from *Solomon* **and** *Joey*, due to their luck-reliant cards. Solomon uses Ordeal of Traveler, and eventually either assembles Exodia or gets out Guardian Sphinx to control the game. Joey uses almost every dice based card in addition to his signature Time Wizard. This makes him *more* danger-ous than Solomon, whose strategies clash a bit (Exodia pieces build in his

hand, making Ordeal less useful). With Joey, you'll often be a dice roll or coin flip away from destruction, and even though he is often as well, as a whole you'll get the worst of it.

Puzzling Experience

You can't actually raise your duel-ist level by completing the puzzles at the card shop, but you **can** earn Kaiba Points to get cards. The Puzzles will get progressively more challenging, and many will have extra cards that don't need to be or even can't be used to finish. If you hit a rough spot, try reading the cards **very carefully**. If you are still stumped, just begin experimenting and keep reading and thinking: a lot of times it will be some-thing fairly simple that is the difference between solving the puzzle and being 500 damage points shy. Also remem-ber that many times you won't deplete Solomon's LP exactly (you'll often have a slight overkill).

Video Game Reviews

Running Into A Brick Wall

If an opponent is giving you a really hard time, make sure you are paying attention not only to what but **how** they play. You can make it quite far in this game with a fairly hodgepodge Beatdown deck, adding and subtracting key cards to exploit an opponent's Weakness (like Royal Decree against a Trap heavy deck).

Only Jerks Ask For A Card You Are Using!

In addition to needing to have someone registered to get them to trade with you, you also need to have the card they want. That varies some, and I've seen players ask for an offer many, many different cards in assorted combinations. Also, you need to have **at least one copy of the card** in your trunk in order for them to ask: unlike a lot of real duelists I know, the characters seem to know that if you're using it in your deck, you probably need it.

Shopping Spree!

Save up **at least 300 KP** to spend at the Card Shop south of your house.

Enter it; buy one pack from the desired set. Ideally, it will be all commons. Next, leave the shop and use the Return to House option to safely head home and save. Now return to the shop. **Congratulations:** the rarity schemes for the remaining booster packs of the one you just bought are locked in for the rest of the game day. In other words, you can now open a pack, record the rarity of the cards in it, and if you quit without saving, you can open the pack again and you may get different cards, but of the same rarity. So if you open a pack and its got four commons and a Super Rare you don't want, just reset, come back, and try the pack again: it'll still have four commons and a Super Rare, but there's decent odds they'll be **different cards** than before. New Booster packs appear every two levels you gain until after Level 20. Some packs won't appear until after specific events in the game.

Better Late Than Never...

Once you have collected **at least** 80% of the cards in a set, you'll receive a set list. This is mainly useful as an indicator of whether to bother finishing out a set or to move onto another one. Surprisingly, it is worth collecting the early packs as they seem to have at least one "good" card (like Pot of Greed in the "Miracles of Nature" booster pack), and at least for that early in the game, some decent beatsticks.

They Came From the Shadows...

If you stay out as late as you can and keep looking, you'll eventually run into **Yami Yugi.** He'll only take time to warn you about the risks of being out so late, and the next day you'll get an e-mail warning you about people being attacked and forced to duel late at night. At this point, once its night time in the game, you run the **risk of being ambushed and forced into a duel.** The opponent will just randomly intercept you on your way to another location on the map. As long as you've built your deck up at least a little, you're only in trouble if you give them several turns to set up. The main problem is that **if you lose here, its Game Over.** On the bright side, because that is the penalty for losing a "Shadow Game", you get 30 extra points just for surviving it. Use the "Head Home" option to safely head home and save, and do it often. Once you've dueled both Dox (one of the "interceptors") and Serenity, Dox will kidnap Serenity and you'll get to rescue her. One last important fact is that as you progress to the second section of map, you'll be intercepted by **different** duelists than on the first portion, and that after you begin the "final" story arc, Rare Hunters will begin intercepting you in addition to guys like Pegasus and Yami Bakura (both of those two will be unlocked by earlier special events). Speaking of Pegasus…

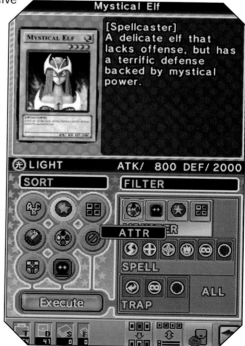

My Pegasus Flew the Coop!

Possibly the **worst** thing about the game is this glitch. Pegasus is one of the duelists who will randomly challenge you, though there is one automatic, unavoidable duel before this happens. If you duel him enough in random encounters, he'll become a regular opponent and stop challenging you at random. If you do this **before** you beat Yami Marik Pegasus will then disappear from the game. Even if you don't enjoy dueling him, trading him is the **only** way to get **Imperial Order,** and of course he is the only source for his deck recipe. So if you want to get them, you either have to duel him enough to get them (the amount varies) before you run into Marik (as Namu), as that is the first of the possible "*trigger*" points. Keep in mind, some won't lose access to Pegasus until the day after that event or until farther in the chain of events. The alternative is to wait until after you've beaten Yami Marik before dueling Pegasus enough to get his mood-indicator

past "-_-". As trading and getting a deck recipe are both semi-random awards, I suggest waiting until after you beat the rest of the game, even though it will take longer.

Enter Low, Win High!

After reaching Level 8 (and rescuing Serenity), you'll eventually get a message notifying you that you've qualified for the **Beginner's Cup** (an e-mail they'll send will tell you when it begins). The tournament won't actually start until you tell Roland you're ready, so just take your time at this point to duel the four duelists in the building (Mokuba, Serenity, Solomon, and Tea), save as needed, and clean out the store that is conveniently located here as well. Since you'll be leveling up while doing this, stick mostly to dueling Serenity and Tea: they won't give as many Experience points, but it is **much easier to earn multiple bonuses** so you'll probably end up with just as many Kaiba Points for pack purchasing as you would dueling Solomon, but with less hassle. This will also keep the packs from horribly out pacing you (as you will end up unlocking quite a few if you follow this strategy through). Whenever you feel your ready (though I wouldn't waste time going past Level 16), go ahead and tell Roland you're ready to begin the tournament. After you win... someone steals the special Prize Pack of cards you'd have one, and the story progresses.

When In Doubt, Wander About.

After this, Kaiba will upgrade your Duel Disk so that it will display a ranking (compared to yourself) of a located duelist (whether Registered or not) as a display of 1-5 stars above

them on the map. Wander around and keep talking to people and dueling and eventually you'll face Bandit Keith, who acts like he is the thief but denies it after you beat him. Once again, continue wandering and eventually you'll find Keith again, **but this time he's with Pegasus.** Duel Pegasus and win in order to get the **3 card Prize Pack.** After this, the preliminaries of the Expert Cup begin. Simply put, this means you can now travel between towns via train. Now get ready to wander around some more because you need to do **two things** to progress.

Once, Twice, Three Times Ishizu

Duel and defeat Ishizu **three times in a row** (she'll probably be the highest ranked duelist on the field). Once you've defeated her three times, you can finally face Yami Bakura... if your Level is high enough (11+). To find Yami Bakura, seek out the normal Bakura at night and challenge him. His dark half will emerge and **the duel is on!**

rit Message "L"

Video Game Reviews

And Now For Something Completely Different... Not!

Once you've beaten Bakura (and are at least at Level 12), the next morning you'll finally be invited to **Expert Cup Finals,** being held at Kaiba's mansion. Except the mansion is locked. Kill time (dueling being the obvious way) until nightfall the next day. Finally Roland will track you down and take you to the mansion. Naturally, since this game has to pretend to at least halfway follow the show, Noa will appear and make life difficult. You'll have to track down (and beat) the Big 5 one by one, defeat Noa, and then Gozaburo will challenge you with a 20 turn time limit. **Lose any of these and it's Game Over.** To make it more challenging, Big 5 Number 5, Noa, and Gozaburo must all be

Solomon
Welcome!

beaten **in a row,** as you can't save in between. You'll get some cards out of this and then have a chance to finally participate in the Expert cup finals. Win there (and get to have fun watching the computer duel itself a little) and you get another Special Prize Pack, the ability to use the **Password Machine** in the Card Shop, to progress further in the story, and to break the rules… well, one rule. You are allowed **one banned card in your deck** from this point forward. Of course, so is everyone else. Go home and sleep to push onto to the final story arc.

Bad Hair Day

Look for Ishizu to be able to battle Kaiba for an Egyptian god Card as mentioned earlier. Now you get to know the joy of random attacks by Rare Hunters at night. After a few duels with them, you'll run into Marik **pretending** to be Namu. He won't duel you yet, but talking to him will progress the story… and if you've gotten chummy with Pegasus, **this is the first chance for his glitch to kick in, so if you didn't take my advice about avoiding him earlier, now you have to duel him like mad to get him to trade you Imperial Order and get his deck list.** Enjoy it, because eventually, he'll just disappear. If you did listen to me and avoided dueling him outside of the one required time, **keep avoiding him for now.** Eventually you'll run into Rare Hunter (the Exodia one with no real name). I guess I

should say he'll run into you. Defeat him, and Marik finally takes over Joey. Beat Marik/Joey to progress the plot, then Marik/Tea, and finally Odion will show up **pretending** to be Marik. Beat Odion then hunt down Joey again to talk, followed by Yami Yugi to find out that you'll have to get a draw game in order to "save Joey". In other words, winning will **still** cause you to lose. Yugi gives you some cards to make it a little easier: **Ring of Destruction and Self-Destruct Button.** After drawing with Joey, Yami Marik finally can be hunted down. When you feel up to it (there's no rush), challenge Yami Marik and **make sure you defeat him using an Egyptian god card.** The final blow to Yami Marik **must** be dealt by **Obelisk or Slifer or else you won't progress to the actual end of the game.**

A Credit To The Game

After beating Yami Marik, the credits roll (and you can play a matching game while they happen), and you are given the choice of saving. **Do so** unless you have a valid reason not to. Now you can enjoy some extras (check your e-mail for two Special Passwords) and have some fun playing the horribly worded survival matches. Level 1 is Mokuba, Seto, Noah, and finally Gozaburo. Level 2 is the Big 5, and Level 3 consists of 5 Rare Hunters and Yami Marik. Defeating each of these gives a token some of Kaiba Points, but more importantly, unlocks some new deck lists. Now enjoy the rest of the game and **finally unlock Pegasus as a full duelist** (you'll have to wander around hoping he'll randomly intercept you at night on Map 2).

Falling Phrase Monster Puzzle

Instructions: Use the letters below the columns to fill in the blocks to form a special phrase. Once you use a letter, cross it off. **Hint:** This is the flavor text of a popular Yu-Gi-Oh! card.

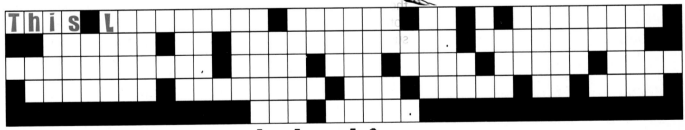

This L

```
            E     E     E O
  V S   L M E   E     D E H D   T A N E   L         O U       F U
  A I N S O E G   C R   V T U R R F G W D   A V   E F R T W E L E H L
I N E I N C I E L N F E A Y R T E A A T N H I I V A D A T E A T T L L
T H W E G I N B E O D A R T S Y R U C L I O N S E V I P C O D R L Y I S
```

When it's not just a game!

Visit www.pojo.com/yu-gi-oh/puzzles.shtml for the answers to this puzzle and other great Yu-Gi-Oh! and trading card game news and fun!

109

Yu-Gi-Oh! Forbidden List Word Search

On the Right Page, we've created a Yu-Gi-Oh! Word Search that lists all 23 cards on the Advanced List Forbidden List.

Can you find them all?

BLACK LUSTER SOLDIER

BUTTERFLY DAGGER

CHANGE OF HEART

CHAOS EMPEROR DRAGON

DELINQUENT DUO

FIBER JAR

GRACEFUL CHARITY

HARPIES FEATHER DUSTER

IMPERIAL ORDER

MAGICAL SCIENTIST

MAKYURA THE DESTRUCTOR

MIRAGE OF NIGHTMARE

MIRROR FORCE

MONSTER REBORN

PAINFUL CHOICE

POT OF GREED

RAIGEKI

RING OF DESTRUCTION

SINISTER SERPENT

THE FORCEFUL SENTRY

TRIBE NFECTING VIRUS

WITCH OF THE BLACK FOREST

YATA GARASU

Y F W M S R D L H S E R B R S Y T C

R I L O A E E M A B R I U E I T S T

T I G N C H E I R V A N T I N I E R

N O R S H Q R R P H M G T D I R R I

E V E T A F G R I R T O E L S A O P

S O D E O Y F O E O H F R O T H F D

L T R R S T O R S T G D F S E C K E

U R O R E E T F F C I E L R R L C L

F I L E M C O O E U N S Y E S U A I

E B A B P I P R A R F T D T E F L N

C E I O E O T C T T O R A S R E B Q

R I R R H R E H S E U G U P C E U

O N E N O C A F E E G C G L E A H E

F F P Q R L E I R D A T E K N R T N

E E M O D U H B D E R I R C T G F T

H C I V R F F E U H I O S A E T O D

T T T P A N O R S T M N V L I T H U

P I Y Z G I E J T A J P Z B X K C O

D N I D O A G A E R M B S Z C U T Q

V G S P N P N R R U O F J N Y D I S

S V T J J D A Z P Y E H Q I E R W K

P I Y K G A H A I K E G I A R L T X

J R O D X F C Z Y A T A G A R A S U

F U X T Z T X F O M H R O Y Z P U T

C S M A G I C A L S C I E N T I S T

Gaia
The Fierce
Knight

How well do you know Gaia The Fierce Knight?
Unscramble the tiles to reveal the "flavor text"
from one of Yugi's favorite cards.

WHO	A KN	VELS	ITH.	IS	E RE
TRA	IS B	A FO	RCE	ATTL	ED W
THAN	TO B	THE	WIN	CKON	E CH
D. H	IGHT	ORSE	SE H	ARGE	FAS
TER					

A KN				

Visit www.pojo.com/yu-gi-oh/puzzles.shtml for the answers to this puzzle and other great Yu-Gi-Oh! and trading card game news and fun!

pojo.com When it's not just a game!